P9-DCV-322

# Seasons

## By Debbie Mumm®

Each changing
season offers its
own joys,
purpose,
and beauty

The fresh new leaves of spring, The colorful joys of summer,
Autumn's spicy splendor, Winter's quiet contentment...
Celebrate the seasons with these beautiful quilts and crafts.

Debbie Mumm®

*Created for Leisure Arts by Debbie Mumm®*

©2005 by Debbie Mumm • Leisure Arts, Inc., 5701 Ranch Drive, Little Rock, AR 72223 www.leisurearts.com

# Dear Friends–

*For all the seasons of the year, for every season of life, quilts are the perfect keepsakes to mark each passage. As the twentieth anniversary of my company quickly approaches, I've been thinking about just how fast time goes by and how quickly each season comes around…and, how important it is to celebrate every moment, every season. What better way to celebrate than with a wonderful assortment of quilts and crafts inspired by the four seasons. And, what a great way to decorate your home for each seasonal change! Soft greens and freshly unfurled leaves typify our springtime quilts. The bold designs and vibrant colors of summer find their way into a playful bed quilt and daisy-decked lap quilt. Spicy colors and textures of autumn are beautiful in lap and wall quilts and a wool table runner. The coziness and quiet contentment of winter are exemplified by a wonderful lap quilt, flannel quilt, and comfy pillows. You'll find a project for every season and every occasion in this beautiful book. Relax, and please don't hurry yourself, as you browse through the pages and projects. I think you'll find the artwork as inspirational as the quilts.*

*Have fun celebrating and decorating for the seasons with these beautiful projects.*

Enjoy! Debbie Mumm
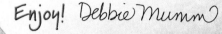

# Contents

# Spring

Spirits soar
and flowers grow
when sweet
spring dances in.

Let your spirits soar with a freshly-
unfurled bed quilt and a wall quilt that
changes with each season.
Decorator pillows and a nesting bird
set the scene for spring.

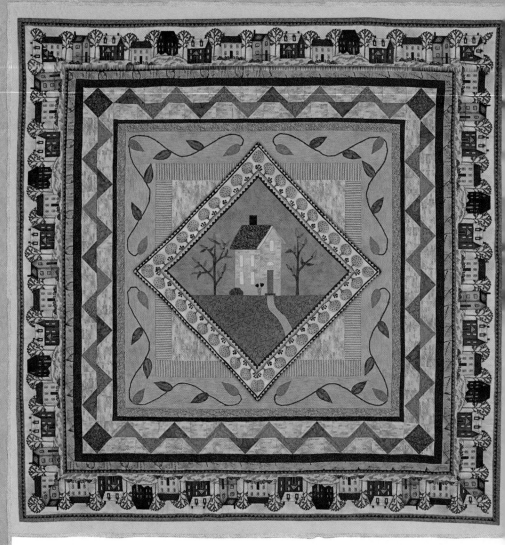

# Changing Seasons Wall Quilt

Finished Size: 62" x 62

A quaint little house changes with each season on this spectacular medallion-style quilt. Medallion centers attach to the larger quilt with hook and loop tape so changing your décor seasonally is as easy as can be. Couched yarn vines and a cobbled path are bordered by a sweet neighborhood of houses. If a house print isn't available, this quilt would be equally charming with a plaid or floral border. The seasonal center panels feature easy appliqués with bead and embroidery embellishments.

# Fabric Requirements and Cutting Instructions

Read all instructions before beginning and use ¼"-wide seam allowances throughout. Read Cutting Strips and Pieces on page 92 prior to cutting fabrics.

| Changing Seasons Wall Quilt 62" x 62" | FIRST CUT | | SECOND CUT | |
|---|---|---|---|---|
| | Number of Strips or Pieces | Dimensions | Number of Pieces | Dimensions |
| **Fabric A** Background & Pieced Fifth Border 1½ yards | 1<br>11 | 22½" x 42"<br>2½" x 42" | 1<br>8<br>152 | 22½" square<br>2½" x 3½"<br>2½" squares |
| **Fabric B** First Border ⅓ yard | 4 | 2½" x 42" | 2<br>2 | 2½" x 26½"<br>2½" x 22½" |
| **Fabric C** Appliquéd Second Border ⅝ yard | 4 | 4½" x 42" | 2<br>2 | 4½" x 34½"<br>4½" x 26½" |
| **Fabric D** Third Border ¼ yard | 4 | 1½" x 42" | 2<br>2 | 1½" x 36½"<br>1½" x 34½" |
| **Fabric E** Fourth & Sixth Borders ⅜ yard | 5<br>4 | 1½" x 42"<br>1" x 42" | 2<br>2 | 1" x 37½"<br>1" x 36½" |
| **Fabric F** Flying Geese ¼ yard each of three fabrics | 2* | 2½" x 42"<br><br>*Cut for each fabric | 16* | 2½" x 4½" |
| **Fabric G** Corner Squares ⅙ yard | 1 | 4½" x 42" | 4 | 4½" square |
| **Fabric H** Seventh Border ¼ yard | 5 | 1½" x 42" | | |
| **Outside Border** 4 yards** | 4 | 66½" x 6½"**<br>(fussy cut) | | |
| **Binding** ⅝ yard | 7 | 2¾" x 42" | | |

**Backing** - 3⅞ yards
**Batting** - 68" x 68"
**Yarn for Vine** - 4 yards
**Leaf Appliqués** - Assorted Scraps
**Lightweight Fusible Web** - ½ yard
**Temporary Fabric Marker**

*\*\*Yardage for this directional fabric will include enough for Changing Season Center Panel tree borders.*
 *For directional fabric, the size that is listed first runs parallel to selvage.*

## Changing Seasons Wall Quilt

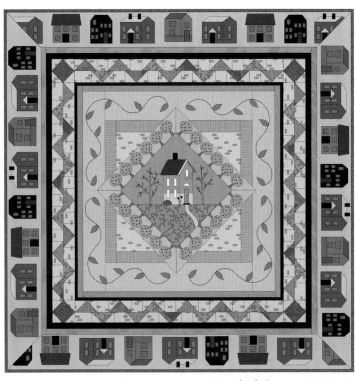

*Finished Size: 62" x 62"*

## Getting Started

Give your room seasonal charm with this Changing Seasons Wall Quilt. The 22" square center panel is attached on point with hook and loop tape making it a breeze to welcome in each season with a different panel. "Spring" is shown in our layout. Instructions for the Spring, Summer, Autumn, and Winter panels are on pages 11, 12, and 13. The border treatment enhances the seasonal theme, with an appliquéd leaf border, pieced Flying Geese border, and an outside house border that finishes the neighborhood. Yardage for the Outside Border also includes the tree border fabric featured on each Seasonal Panel (see fabric ordering information on page 13).

## Making the Wall Quilt

**1.** Sew 22½" Fabric A square between two 2½" x 22½" Fabric B strips. Press seams toward border. Sew this unit between two 2½" x 26½" Fabric B strips. Press.

**2.** Sew unit from step 1 between two 4½" x 26½" Fabric C strips. Press seams toward Fabric B. Sew this unit between two 4½" x 34½" Fabric C strips. Press.

**3.** Sew unit from step 2 between two 1½" x 34½" Fabric D strips. Press seams toward Fabric D. Sew this unit between two 1½" x 36½" Fabric D strips. Press.

**4.** Sew unit from step 3 between two 1" x 36½" Fabric E strips. Press seams toward Fabric D. Sew this unit between two 1" x 37½" Fabric E strips. Press.

**5.** Refer to Quick Corner Triangles on page 92. Sew two 2½" Fabric A squares to one 2½" x 4½" Fabric F piece as shown. Press. Make forty-eight, sixteen of each combination.

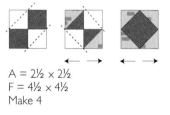

A = 2½ x 2½
F = 2½ x 4½
Make 48
(16 of each combination)

**6.** Arrange and sew together six units from step 5 (two of each combination), five 2½" Fabric A squares and one 2½" x 3½" Fabric A piece as shown. Press. Make four.

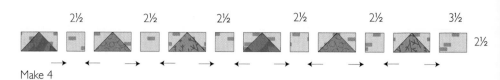

Make 4

**7.** Arrange and sew together one 2½" x 3½" Fabric A piece, six units from step 5 (two of each combination), and five 2½" Fabric A squares as shown. Press. Make four.

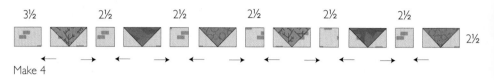

Make 4

**8.** Arrange and sew together one row each from steps 6 and 7. Press. Make four.

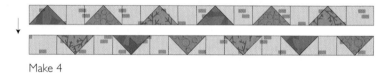

Make 4

**9.** Referring to photo on page 6 and layout on page 9, sew quilt top between two units from step 8. Press seams towards center.

**10.** Making quick corner triangle units, sew four 2½" Fabric A squares to one 4½" Fabric G square. Press. Make four.

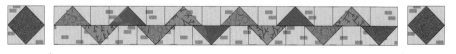

A = 2½ x 2½
F = 4½ x 4½
Make 4

**11.** Sew one unit from step 8 between two units from step 10 as shown. Press. Make two.

Make 2

**12.** Sew quilt top between two units from step 11 as shown. Press.

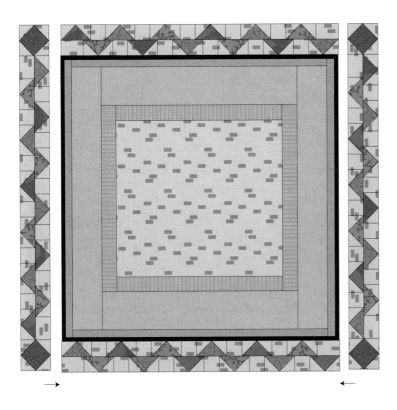

**13.** Sew 1½" x 42" Fabric E strips end-to-end to make one continuous 1½"-wide strip. Referring to Adding the Borders on page 94, measure quilt through center from side to side. Cut two 1½"-wide Fabric E strips to that measurement. Sew to top and bottom of quilt. Press seams toward Fabric E.

**14.** Measure quilt through center from top to bottom, including borders just added. Cut two 1½"-wide Fabric E strips to that measurement. Sew to sides of quilt. Press.

**15.** Refer to steps 13 and 14 to join, measure, trim, and sew 1½"-wide Fabric H strips to top, bottom, and sides of quilt. Press.

**16.** Refer to Mitered Borders on page 94. Sew 66½" x 6½" Fabric H strips to top, bottom and sides of quilt, mitering corners. Press seam toward the Outside Border.

## Adding the Appliqués

Refer to appliqué instruction on page 93. Our instructions are for Quick-Fuse Appliqué, but if you prefer hand appliqué, add ¼" seam allowances.

**1.** Refer to photo and layout on pages 6 and 7, Couching Technique on page 95, and Vine Design on page 15. Using temporary fabric marker, draw vine on Fabric C (Second Border). Couch yarn following drawn lines.

**2.** Refer to Quick-Fuse Appliqué on page 93. Using Leaf pattern on page 15, trace twenty-eight leaves on paper side of fusible web. Use assorted scraps to prepare leaves for fusing. Refer to photo and layout on pages 6 and 7 to arrange and fuse leaves to border. Finish appliqué edges with machine satin stitch or other decorative stitching as desired.

## Finishing the Quilt

**1.** Cut backing crosswise into two equal pieces. Sew pieces together to make one 70" x 80" (approximate) backing piece.

**2.** Arrange and baste backing, batting, and top together, referring to Layering the Quilt on page 94. Hand or machine quilt as desired.

**3.** Sew 2¾" x 42" binding strips end-to-end to make one continuous 2¾"-wide strip. Refer to Binding the Quilt on page 95 and bind quilt to finish.

Spring

Summer

Autumn

Winter

# Changing Seasons
## Center Panels

Each Center Panel
Finished Size: 22" x 22"

Tiny bead buds, crystals for sprinkler spray, beads for apples—
have fun embellishing these easy medallion center squares for the
Changing Seasons Wall Quilt. Houses use the same appliqués but
are distinguished by colors and textures. Seasonal accessories
like a vase of tulips, a sprinkler, a basket of apples, and a
snowman make each medallion center a symbol of the season.
A border of seasonal trees finishes each medallion center.

# Fabric Requirements and Cutting Instructions

Read all instructions before beginning and use ¼"-wide seam allowances throughout. Read Cutting Strips and Pieces on page 92 prior to cutting fabrics.

| Each Changing Season Center Panel 22" x 22" | FIRST CUT | |
|---|---|---|
| | Number of Strips or Pieces | Dimensions |
| **Fabric Needed for One Panel:** | | |
| Fabric A ½ yard | 1 | 16½" square |
| Fabric B ⅜ yard | 1 | 12½" square |
| **BORDER** | | |
| Outside Border 1⅝ yards* | 4* | 29" x 3½" |

Backing - ¾ yard
Batting - 26" x 26"
Appliqués - Assorted Scraps
Lightweight Fusible Web - ¾ yard
Stabilizer - ¾ yard
Embroidery Floss - Green and orange
Beads - 20 for Spring Tree, 39 for Summer Sprinkler Spray, 6 for Autumn Apples, 8 for Winter Snowman

*Enough yardage is provided in the Changing Seasons Wall Quilt, this yardage requirement is only needed if making just Center Panel.*

## Changing Seasons Center Panels

*Spring Season*

*Summer Season*

*Autumn Season*

*Winter Season*

# Making the Center Panel

**1.** Refer to Quick Corner Triangles on page 92. Sew one 12½" Fabric B square to one 16½" Fabric A square as shown. Press.

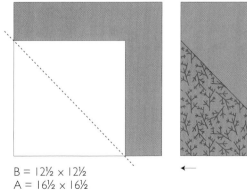

B = 12½ × 12½
A = 16½ × 16½

**2.** Refer to Mitered Borders on page 94. Sew 29" x 3½" seasonal tree Outside Border strips to top, bottom and sides of quilt, mitering corners. Press seams toward border.

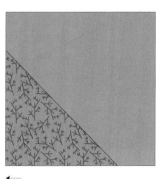

## Adding the Appliqués

Refer to appliqué instructions on page 93. Our instructions are for Quick-Fuse Appliqué, but if you prefer hand appliqué, reverse patterns and add ¼" seam allowances. We recommend using stabilizer for machine appliqué.

## Spring House Quilt

**1.** Refer to Quick-Fuse Appliqué on page 93 and appliqué patterns on pages 14, 15, and 16. Trace all patterns on page 14, path on page 15, and spring trees and leaves on page 16 onto paper side of fusible web. Use assorted scraps to prepare appliqués for fusing.

**2.** Referring to photo and layout on pages 10 and 11, position and fuse pieces to quilt. Finish appliqué edges with machine satin stitch or other decorative stitching as desired.

**3.** Referring to Embroidery Stitch Guide on page 95 and tulip pattern on page 14, use three strands of embroidery floss and a stem stitch to stitch tulip stems to quilt.

## Finishing the Center Panel

**1.** Place 26" x 26" backing piece right sides together with quilt top and place on batting. Stitch around all sides ¼" from raw edges of quilt top leaving 4" opening for turning. Trim batting close to stitching, clip corners, turn, press, and hand stitch opening closed.

**2.** Hand or machine quilt as desired.

**3.** Refer to photo and layout on pages 10 and 11 and detail photo below to arrange and sew beads to trees as desired. Add any additional embellishment.

**4.** Position and hand sew "hook" (rough) section of hook and loop tape to each corner on back of center panel. Pin panel to Changing Seasons Wall Quilt to determine "loop" placement. Hand sew loop tape in place.

## Summer Center Panel

**1.** Make the summer panel top following instructions on page 11 using the summer tree border strips as the Outside Border.

**2.** Refer to Quick-Fuse Appliqué on page 93 and appliqué patterns on pages 14, 15, and 17. Trace house, bush, path, sprinkler, and summer trees onto paper side of fusible web. Use assorted scraps to prepare appliqués for fusing.

**3.** Referring to photo and layout on pages 10 and 11, position and fuse pieces to quilt. Finish appliqué edges with machine satin stitch or other decorative stitching as desired.

**4.** Refer to Finishing the Quilt steps 1 and 2, to finish edges and quilt top.

**5.** Referring to photo below, arrange and sew beads to make sprinkler spray.

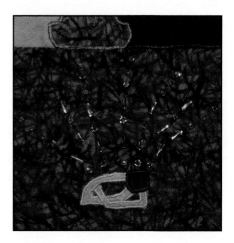

## Autumn Center Panel

**1.** Make the autumn panel top following instructions on page 11 using the autumn tree border strips as the Outside Border.

**2.** Refer to Quick-Fuse Appliqué on page 93 and appliqué patterns on pages 14, 15, and 16. Trace house, bush, path, apple barrel, three leaf piles, fall trees, and leaves onto paper-side of fusible web. Use assorted scraps to prepare appliqués for fusing.

**3.** Referring to photo and layout on pages 10 and 11, position and fuse pieces to quilt. Finish appliqué edges with machine satin stitch or other decorative stitching as desired.

**4.** Refer to Finishing the Quilt steps 1 and 2, to finish edges and quilt top.

**5.** Referring to Apple Barrel pattern and photo below, arrange and sew beads for apples.

## Winter Center Panel

**1.** Make the winter quilt following instructions on page 11 using the winter tree border strips as the Outside Border.

**2.** Refer to Quick-Fuse Appliqué on page 93 and appliqué patterns on pages 14, 15, and 16. Trace house, bush, path, snowman, two snow mounds, icicles, tree snow, bush snow, and winter trees onto paper-side of fusible web. Use assorted scraps to prepare appliqués for fusing.

**3.** Referring to photo and layout on pages 10 and 11, position and fuse pieces to quilt. Finish appliqué edges with machine satin stitch or other decorative stitching as desired.

**4.** Refer to Finishing the Quilt steps 1 and 2, to finish edges and quilt top.

**5.** Referring to Snowman pattern on page 15 and photo below, arrange and sew beads on snowman.

**6.** Referring to Embroidery Stitch Guide on page 95, use three strands of embroidery floss and a satin stitch to stitch snowman nose.

—Tip—
### Spring Into Action!

Houses and all the tree borders are on the same fabric, 67146-475, Through the Seasons Stripe by South Sea Imports®. Look for it at your local quilt shop or order online at www.debbiemumm.com or call toll free 866-Get-Mumm. You will need 4 yards to make the Changing Seasons Wall Quilt which includes the four seasonal tree borders for center panels.

House
Chimney

14

## Changing Seasons
## Center Panel Patterns

*Patterns are reversed for use
with Quick-Fuse Appliqué (page 93).*

Tracing Line ———————
Tracing Line - - - - - - - - - -
*(will be hidden behind other fabrics)*
Embroidery Line .......................
Bead Placement .......................

Summer Sprinkler Pattern

Autumn Apple Barrel Pattern

Path

Winter Tree
Snow Pattern
Make 5

Winter Bush Snow Pattern

Winter Snowman Pattern

**Suggested Vine Design for
Changing Seasons Wall Quilt**

Winter Snow Mound and
Fall Leaf Pile Pattern

Winter Snow Mound and
Fall Leaf Pile Pattern

House Icicle Pattern

**Changing Seasons Wall Quilt**
Vine Leaf
Make 28

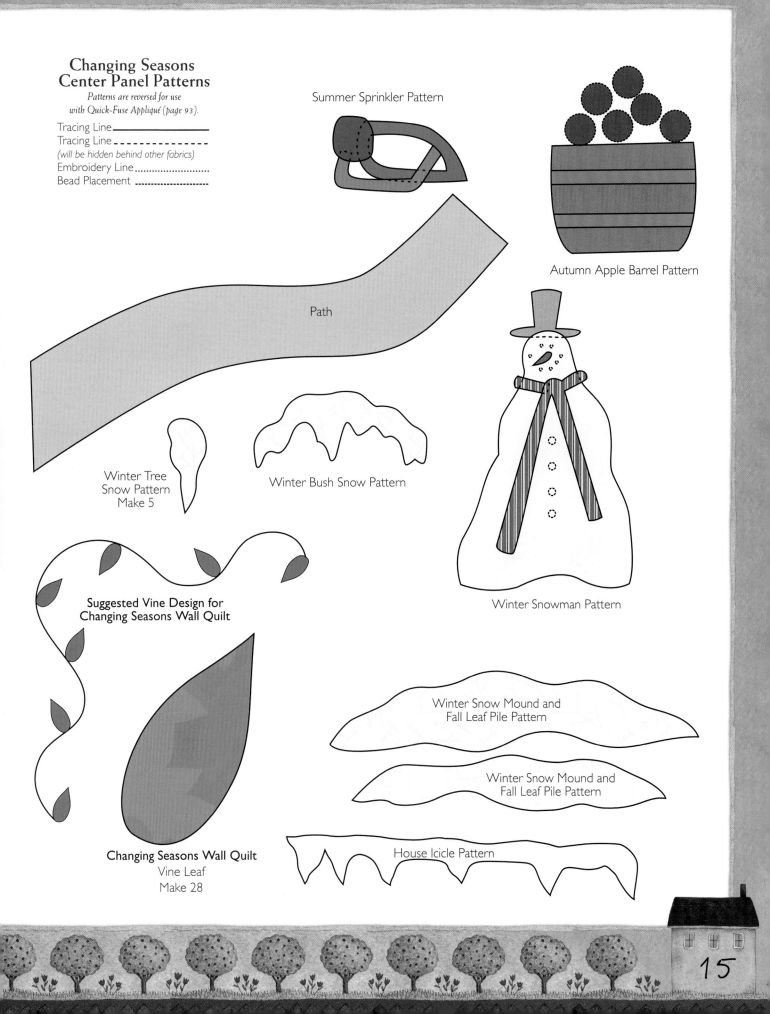

Spring Center Panel Trees
Autumn and Winter Tree Trunks

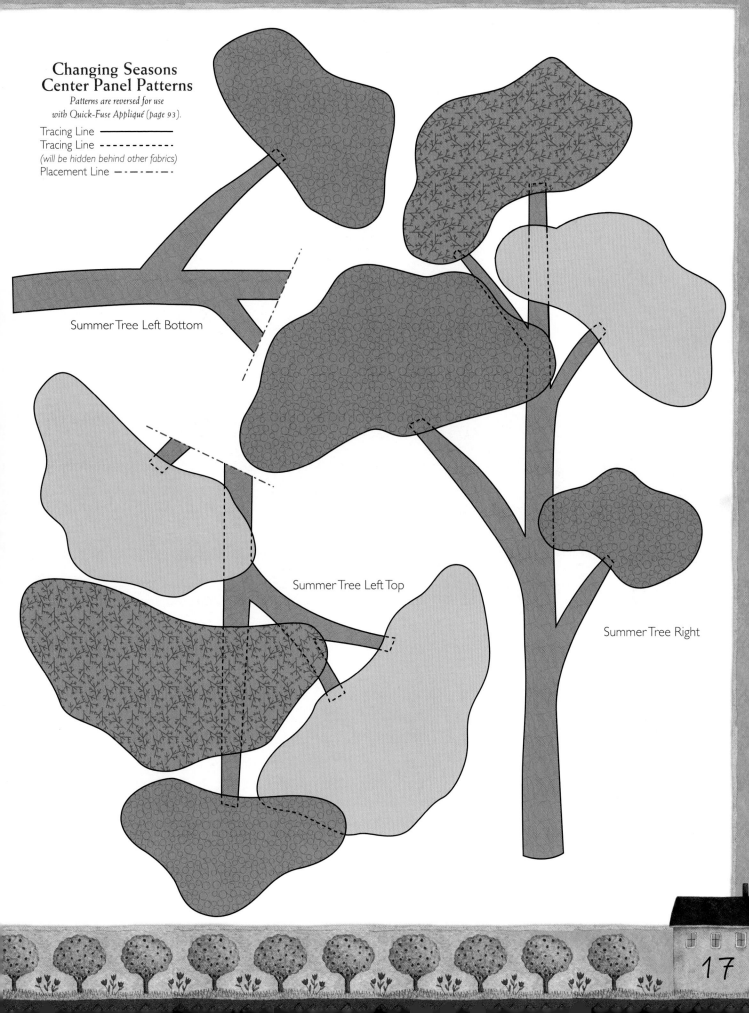

## Changing Seasons
## Center Panel Patterns

*Patterns are reversed for use*
*with Quick-Fuse Appliqué (page 93).*

Tracing Line ─────────
Tracing Line ─ ─ ─ ─ ─ ─
*(will be hidden behind other fabrics)*
Placement Line ─·─·─·─

Summer Tree Left Bottom

Summer Tree Left Top

Summer Tree Right

17

# Fresh Foliage Bed Quilt

**Quick!**

*Finished Size: 84" x 108*

Simple and beautiful, this quilt uses striped fabrics and easy
leaf appliqués to create a decorator look for your bed.
Easy enough for a beginner, the over-sized blocks are arranged
to alternate lights and darks and stripe directions. A touch
of brown accents the green and tan color combination.
A variety of pillows complete this beautiful ensemble.

# Fabric Requirements and Cutting Instructions

Read all instructions before beginning and use ¼"-wide seam allowances throughout. Read Cutting Strips and Pieces on page 92 prior to cutting fabrics.

| Fresh Foliage Bed Quilt 84" x 108" | FIRST CUT | | SECOND CUT | |
|---|---|---|---|---|
| | Number of Strips or Pieces | Dimensions | Number of Pieces | Dimensions |
| **Fabric A** Tan Background 1⅛ yards | 3 | 12½" x 42" | 9 | 12½" squares |
| **Fabric B** Striped Background 1⅛ yards | 3 | 12½" x 42" | 9 | 12½" squares |
| **Fabric C** Horizontal Striped Block 2⅙ yards | 6 | 12½" x 42" | 17 | 12½" squares |
| **BORDERS** | | | | |
| **First Border** ⅓ yard | 8 | 1" x 42" | | |
| **Second Border** ⅝ yard | 8 | 2½" x 42" | | |
| **Third Border** ½ yard | 8 | 1½" x 42" | | |
| **Outside Border** 2¼ yards | 9 | 8½" x 42" | | |
| **Binding** ⅞ yard | 10 | 2¾" x 42" | | |

Backing - 7⅞ yards
Batting - 92" x 116"
Oak Appliqué - ⅙ yard **each** of two fabrics
Elm Appliqué - ⅙ yard **each** of two fabrics
White Oak Appliqué - ⅙ yard **each** of two fabrics
Maple Appliqué - ⅓ yard
Sycamore Appliqué - ¼ yard
Lightweight Fusible Web - 1¾ yards

## Getting Started

This quilt consists of thirty-five large blocks measuring 12½" square unfinished. Seventeen of the blocks feature a striped fabric embellished only by quilting and placed horizontally. Eighteen blocks are quick-fuse appliquéd with spring leaves on two different fabrics. The appliquéd blocks use a random color scheme and arrangement and alternate with striped blocks.

## Fresh Foliage Bed Quilt

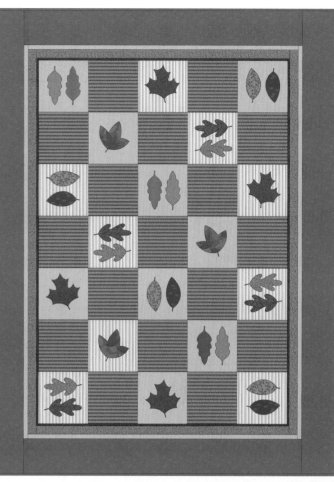

*Finished Size: 84" x 108"*

If you choose to use just one background for the appliquéd blocks, you will need 2⅙ yards of Fabric A to cut eighteen squares and eliminate Fabric B. The leaves are appliquéd prior to sewing the blocks together. The blocks are then sewn together in rows to make a quickly pieced top.

Refer to Accurate Seam Allowance on page 92. Whenever possible, use the Assembly Line Method on page 92. Press seams in direction of arrows.

## Making the Top

Refer to appliqué instructions on page 93. Our instructions are for Quick-Fuse Appliqué, but if you prefer hand appliqué, add ¼"-wide seam allowances.

1. Refer to Quick Fuse Appliqué on page 93 and trace leaf patterns on pages 20-23. Trace the number of appliqués indicated on paper side of fusible web. Using leaf appliqué fabrics prepare appliqués for fusing. Refer to photo and layout on pages 18 and 19, and diagram below, to position and fuse leaves on 12½" Fabric A squares for a total of nine squares. Finish appliqué edges with machine satin stitch or decorative stitching as desired.

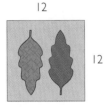

12

12

Make 9
2 with Elm
2 with Maple
3 with White Oak
2 with Sycamore

2. Referring to photo and layout on pages 18 and 19, and diagram, appliqué leaves on 12½" Fabric B squares for a total of nine squares. Finish appliqué edges with machine satin stitch or decorative stitching as desired.

12

12

Make 9
4 with Oak
2 with Elm
2 with Maple
1 with Sycamore

3. Arrange and sew three appliquéd units, (two from step 1, one from step 2,) and two 12½" Fabric C squares as shown to make row 1. Press. Referring to photo and layout on pages 18 and 19, make three more horizontal rows. Press.

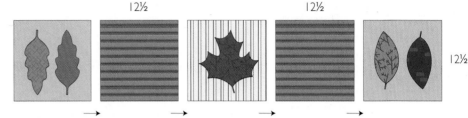

12½  12½  12½

Make 4
(one of each combination)

4. Arrange and sew three 12½" Fabric C squares, and two appliquéd units (one from step 1, one from step 2) as shown. Press. Referring to photo and layout on pages 18 and 19, make two more horizontal rows. Press.

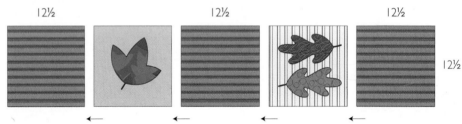

12½  12½  12½  12½

Make 3
(one of each combination)

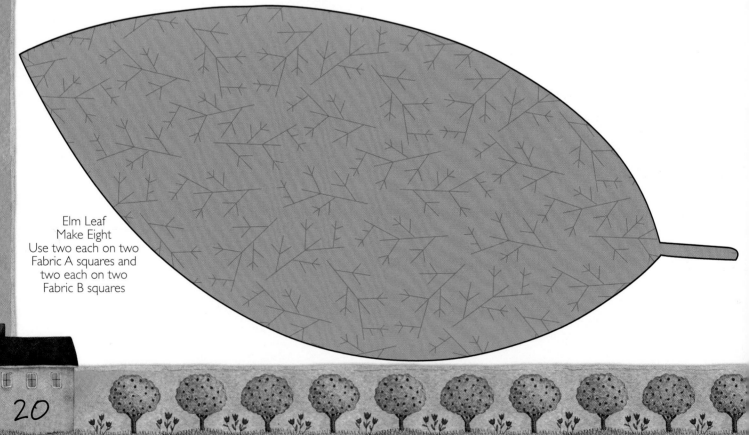

Elm Leaf
Make Eight
Use two each on two
Fabric A squares and
two each on two
Fabric B squares

**5.** Referring to photo and layout on pages 18 and 19, arrange rows from steps 3 and 4 in seven horizontal rows alternating them as shown. Sew rows together. Press.

## Adding the Borders

**1.** Sew 1" x 42" First Border strips end-to-end to make one continuous 1"-wide strip. Press. Refer to Adding the Borders on page 94. Measure quilt through center from side to side. Cut two 1"-wide First Border strips to that measurement. Sew to top and bottom of quilt. Press seams toward border.

**2.** Measure quilt through center from top to bottom including borders just added. Cut two 1"-wide First Border strips to that measurement. Sew to sides of quilt. Press.

**3.** Refer to steps 1 and 2 to join, measure, trim, and sew 2½"-wide Second Border, 1½"-wide Third Border, and 8½"-wide Outside Border strips to top, bottom, and sides of quilt. Press seams toward each newly added border strip.

## Layering and Finishing

**1.** Cut backing crosswise into three equal pieces. Sew pieces together to make one 92" x 120" (approximate) backing piece. Press.

**2.** Arrange and baste backing, batting, and top together referring to Layering the Quilt on page 94. Hand or machine quilt as desired.

**3.** Sew 2¾" binding strips end-to-end to make one continuous 2¾"-wide strip. Refer to Binding the quilt on page 95 and bind quilt to finish.

**Fresh Foliage**
**Bed Quilt Patterns**
*Patterns are reversed for use*
*with Quick-Fuse Appliqué (page 93).*

Tracing Line_____

Sycamore Leaf
Make Three
Use one each on two
Fabric A squares and one
on one Fabric B square

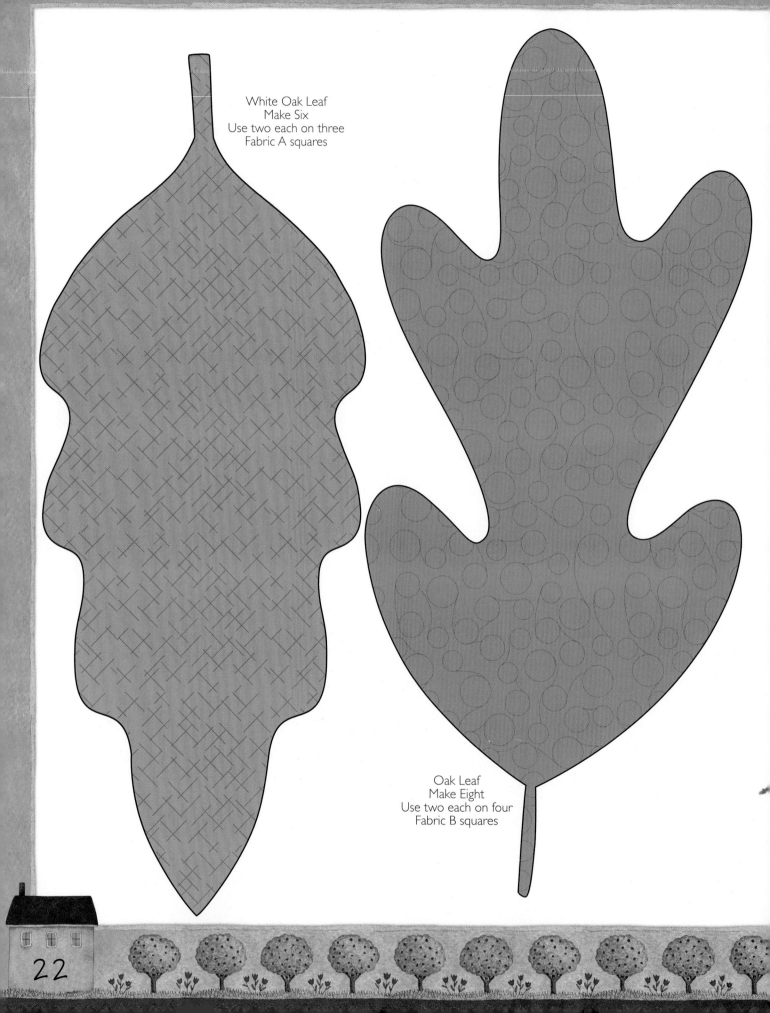

White Oak Leaf
Make Six
Use two each on three
Fabric A squares

Oak Leaf
Make Eight
Use two each on four
Fabric B squares

# Fresh Foliage
# Bed Quilt Patterns

*Patterns are reversed for use
with Quick-Fuse Appliqué (page 93).*

Tracing Line——————————

Maple Leaf
Make Four
Use one each on two Fabric A squares and
one each on two Fabric B squares

# Fresh Foliage
## Pillow Sham
## & Decorator
## Pillows

*Finished Size Pillow Sham: 20" x 30*
*Finished Size Decorator Pillow: 18" x 18*
*Finished Size Sycamore Pillow: 16" x 16*

Create a decorator look in your bedroom by making shams and pillows to coordinate with the Fresh Foliage Bed Quilt. Take a break from appliqué by using a simple stamp to add a leaf motif to the sham border. Striped fabric sews into squares for the decorator pillows that are accented by bias-cut piping. A single leaf becomes the center of attention when highlighted by mitered borders on the accent pillow.

24

# Fabric Requirements and Cutting Instructions

Read all instructions before beginning. Read Cutting Strips and Pieces on page 92 prior to cutting fabrics.

| Fresh Foliage Sham 20" x 30" | FIRST CUT | | SECOND CUT | |
|---|---|---|---|---|
| | Number of Strips or Pieces | Dimensions | Number of Pieces | Dimensions |
| **FOR ONE SHAM** | | | | |
| ■ **Fabric A** Background and Backing 1⅞ yards | 3 | 20½" x 42" | 2 | 20½" x 36½" *(backing)* |
| | | | 1 | 20½" x 25" |
| | | | 1 | 20½" x 1" |
| ▢ **Fabric B** Stamped Border ⅙ yard | 3 | 4½" x 5½" *(cut after stamping)* | | |
| ▤ **Fabric C** Striped Border ⅙ yard* | 1 | 5½" x 42"* | 2 | 5½" x 4½" |
| ■ **Fabric D** Accent Border ⅛ yard | 1 | 1½" x 20½" | | |

Lining - ¾ yard (One 24½" x 34½" piece)
Batting - ¾ yard (One 24½" x 34½" piece)
Green Fabric Ink
Rubber Foam or Stamp
Paper Disposable Plate or Paper Palette
Freezer Paper

*For directional fabric, the size that is listed first runs parallel to selvage (strip width).*

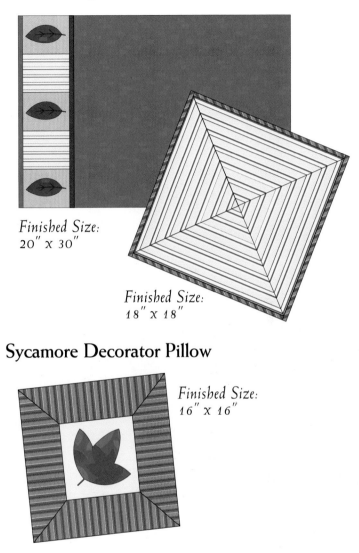

### Fresh Foliage Sham and Decorator Pillows

*Finished Size:*
20" x 30"

*Finished Size:*
18" x 18"

### Sycamore Decorator Pillow

*Finished Size:*
16" x 16"

# Fresh Foliage Pillow Sham

## Getting Started

This pillow sham is edged with alternating hand-stamped and striped fabrics. Appliqués or stenciling could substitute for the stamping. It is recommended to use scraps to practice hand-stamping prior to stamping and cutting Fabric B.

## Stamping Fabric

**1.** Tape freezer paper to counter top or table, waxed side up. Place Fabric B over freezer paper and tape in place. Place a small amount of paint on disposable plate or paper palette. Spread paint to encompass an area large enough for stamp. Dip stamp in paint. Blot stamp on freezer paper to evenly distribute paint. Stamp design on Fabric B. Repeat stamping process to make three sections approximately 6" x 7". Follow paint manufacturer's instructions for drying and setting paint.

**2.** Referring to photo and layout, cut stamped fabric into three 4½" x 5½" stamped pieces centering a leaf in each piece.

**3.** Arrange and sew three units from step 2 and two 5½" x 1½" Fabric C pieces as shown. Press.

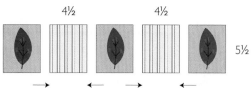

4½           4½

5½

**4.** Fold 1½" x 20½" Fabric D strip in half lengthwise and press to make mock piping. Referring to photo and layout on pages 24 and 25 and with right sides together and matching raw edges, position and sew strip to bottom edge of unit from step 3. Do not press.

**5.** Referring to photo and layout on pages 24 and 25, sew unit from step 4 between 20½" x 1" and 20½" x 25" Fabric A pieces. Press seams toward unit from step 4.

**6.** Layer 24½" x 34½" batting piece between pillow sham top and 24½" x 34½" backing piece. Baste. Hand or machine quilt as desired. Trim batting and lining even with pillow sham top.

**7.** Fold 20½" x 36½" Fabric A backing pieces in half crosswise to measure 20½" x 18¼". Press. Place backing pieces together so folds overlap and backing unit measures the same as pillow sham top. Baste backing pieces together at top and bottom of overlaps.

**8.** With right sides together, position and pin pillow sham top to backing. Using ¼"-wide seam, sew around edges. Trim corners, turn right side out, and press. Insert pillow.

# Fresh Foliage Decorator Pillow

## Materials for One Pillow

Fabric A (Pillow Front and Back) - 1½ yards
Fabric B (Bias Piping) - ⅝ yard
    One 18" square cut into 3"-wide bias strips
Lining - 1¼ yard, two 22" squares (optional)
Batting - Two 22" squares (optional)
½" Cording - 2½ yards
Polyester Fiberfill

*Finished Size: 18" x 18"*

## Getting Started

Triangles fussy cut from striped fabric and bias-cut piping create a dramatic design for an 18" square (finished) pillow.

## Making the Pillow

**1.** To make triangle patterns, draw a 14¼" square on paper. Draw one diagonal line from corner to corner. Diagonal line should measure 20½". Cut to make two triangles. Label one pattern "Pillow Front" and the other "Pillow Back". To speed the cutting process, cut two of each pattern.

**2.** Place triangles on Fabric A as shown. Lightly mark position of two stripes on pattern so the pattern can be placed in the same position for the second cut. Cut four Pillow Fronts and four Pillow Backs.

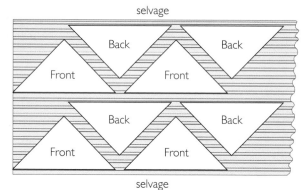

selvage

Back    Back

Front    Front

Back    Back

Front    Front

selvage

**3.** Using a ¼"-wide seam allowance, sew two Pillow Front triangles together as shown. Press. Make two. Sew units together as shown. Press, twisting seams at center (page 77). Repeat step to make pillow back. Square units to 19".

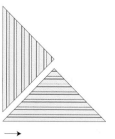

Make 4
(2 of each combination)

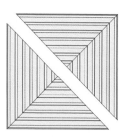

Make 2
(1 of each combination)
Square to 19"

**4.** Refer to Finishing the Pillows, step 1, on page 95 to quilt pillow if desired.

## Making the Piping

**1.** We used bias strips for our piping. Refer to Making Bias Strips on page 94. Start with an 18" square to cut bias strips. Approximately 80" of 3"-wide bias strip is needed to make piping.

**2.** With fabric right side out, cover cording with bias strip of fabric. Use a zipper foot to machine baste close to cording to make piping. Trim seam allowance ½" away from stitches.

**3.** Pin and baste piping to right side of Pillow Front aligning raw edges. Do not baste first and last two inches of cording. Remove 1½" of stitches on one end of cord covering. Trim cording, but not cord covering at intersection of ends. Cord ends should butt against each other, but not overlap. Fold under ½" on one end of cording cover and overlap other end to make a finished seam. Piping will curve more easily at corners if piping seam allowance is clipped at corner and at ¼" intervals just beyond corner.

**4.** Place and pin Pillow Back right sides together with Pillow Front. Using ½"-wide seam, sew around edges leaving a 5" opening for turning and stuffing. Clip corners, turn, and press.

**5.** Stuff to desired fullness with polyester fiberfill. Hand stitch opening closed.

# Sycamore Decorator Pillow

## Materials for One Pillow

Fabric A (Background) - ¼ yard
    One 8½" square
Border and Backing - ⅝ yard
    Two 11" x 16½" pieces (Backing)
    Four 4½" x 20" pieces
Leaf Appliqué - Scrap
Lightweight Fusible Web - ¼ yard
Lining - 20" square
Batting - 20" square
16" Pillow Form

*Finished Size: 16" x 16"*

## Getting Started

Borders with mitered corners highlight an appliquéd leaf center square. This pillow is fast to make and will look great on a bed covered with our Fresh Foliage Bed Quilt or as a splash of color in a sunroom or family room. Refer to appliqué instructions on page 93. Our instructions are for Quick-Fuse Appliqué, but if you prefer hand appliqué, add ¼"-wide seam allowance.

## Making the Pillow

**1.** Refer to Quick-Fuse Appliqué on page 93 and Sycamore Leaf Pattern on page 21. Trace leaf on paper side of fusible web. Using Leaf Appliqué scrap prepare appliqué for fusing.

**2.** Referring to photo, position and fuse leaf to 8½" Fabric A square. Finish appliqué edge with machine satin stitch or other decorative stitch as desired.

**3.** Refer to Mitered Borders on page 94. Sew 4½" x 20" Border strips to top, bottom, and sides of unit from step 2, adjusting position of Border strip to match stripes. Miter corners. Press seams toward border.

**4.** Refer to Finishing Pillows, page 95, step 1, to quilt pillow top. Refer to steps 2-4 to sew 11" x 16½" Backing pieces to pillow. Insert 16" pillow form.

# Early Bird Wall Quilt

Finished Size depends on Finishir

*The early bird gets the quilt done first! Especially when it's as cute and easy as this one! Diagonal bands of color create a springtime sky for this appliquéd bird. Our little wren built her nest with couched yarns, fabric, and feathers for a touch of whimsy. Complete your project with a frame like we did or add borders and binding.*

# Fabric Requirements and Cutting Instructions

Read all instructions before beginning and use ¼"-wide seam allowances throughout. Read Cutting Strips and Pieces on page 92 prior to cutting fabrics.

| Early Bird Wall Quilt 14" x 25½" | FIRST CUT | | SECOND CUT | |
|---|---|---|---|---|
| | Number of Strips or Pieces | Dimensions | Number of Pieces | Dimensions |
| **Fabric A** Yellow Background ¼ yard | 1 | 5½" x 42" | 1 1 | 5½" x 11½" 4½" x 8½" |
| **Fabric B** Gold Background ⅛ yard | 1 | 2½" x 42" | 1 1 | 2½" x 15½" 2½" x 12½" |
| **Fabric C** Lt Blue Background ¼ yard | 2 | 2½" x 42" | 1 1 | 2½" x 25½" 2½" x 16½" |
| **Fabric D** Med Lt Blue Background ¼ yard | 2 | 2½" x 42" | 1 1 | 2½" x 25½" 2½" x 20½" |
| **Fabric E** Med Blue Background ¼ yard | 2 | 2½" x 42" | 1 1 | 2½" x 24½" 2½" x 23½" |
| **Fabric F** Dk Blue Background ¼ yard | 2 | 2½" x 42" | 1 1 | 2½" x 25½" 2½" x 19½" |
| **Fabric G** Dk Green Checks ¼ yard | 2 | 2" x 42" | 2 1 2 | 2" x 22" 2" x 17½" 1½" x 6½" |
| **Fabric H** Green Checks ⅙ yard | 2 | 2" x 42" | 2 | 2" x 22" |

Backing - ¾ yard
Batting - 23" x 34"
**Bird Beak, Wing, and Body** - Assorted Scraps
Nest - Scrap
Fusible Web - ⅙ yard
See-Through Ruler
Assorted Yarns for Nest
Feathers for Nest
Black Embroidery Floss
Temporary Marker
Frame (14" x 25½" opening)
Mounting Board (to fit frame)
Masking Tape

## Early Bird Wall Quilt

*Inside Frame Dimension: 14" x 25½"*

## Getting Started

This quilt features a background sky that is strip-pieced on grain and cut at an angle to make a striking diagonal background. Strip piecing is also used to create easy checks to form a leaf base for the bird nest. The stylized bird and nest are quick-fused.

Couched yarn and other embellishments are added to the nest. A choice of finishing options is included in the instructions. Frame it like ours, or add borders and binding for a more traditional approach if desired.

# Making the Quilt

**1.** Arrange and sew together 5½" x 11½" Fabric A, 2½" x 15½" Fabric B, 2½" x 19½" Fabric F, and 2½" x 23½" Fabric E pieces, staggering each fabric piece two inches as shown to make Unit 1. Press.

**Unit 1**

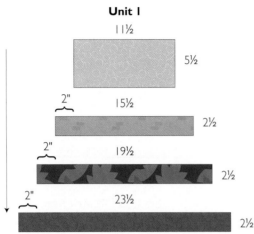

**2.** Arrange and sew together 2½" x 25½" Fabric D, 2½" x 25½" Fabric C, 2½" x 25½" Fabric F, 2½" x 24½" Fabric E, 2½" x 20½" Fabric D, 2½" x 16½" Fabric C, 2½" x 12½" Fabric B, and 4½" x 8½" Fabric A pieces, staggering each fabric piece two inches as shown to make Unit 2. Press.

**Unit 2**

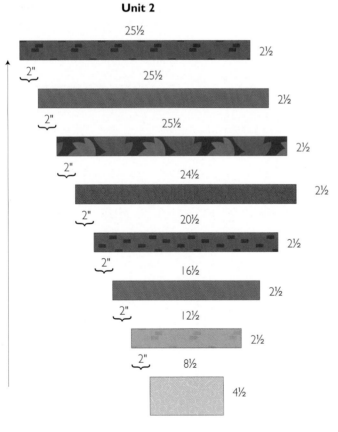

**3.** Referring to diagram in step 4, sew Unit 1 to Unit 2 matching raw edges. Press seam toward Unit 1.

**4.** Using a see through ruler and temporary marker, place ruler along top edge of background and draw a straight line along seam edges of unit from step 3 as shown starting at intersections of Unit 1 and Unit 2. The seams will be at a 45° angle to ruler.

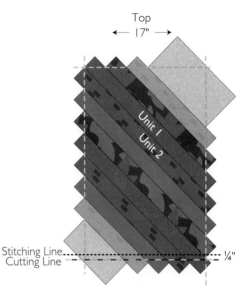

**5.** Referring to diagram in step 4, place see through ruler along side edge of background perpendicular to marked line at top of background. Using a temporary maker, draw a line along seam edges on left and right sides of background, distance should be 17" apart.

**6.** Place see through ruler along bottom edge of background perpendicular to sides. Referring to diagram in step 4, draw a line across bottom of background with temporary marker; this will be the stitching line. Place ruler ¼" away from drawn line and cut along bottom edge as shown in step 4.

**7.** Sew two 2" x 22" Fabric G and two 2" x 22" Fabric H strips together alternating as shown to make a strip set. Press. Cut ten 2"- wide segments.

22

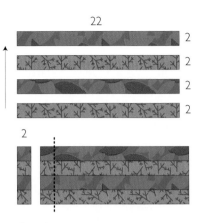

2
2
2
2

2

Cut 10 segments

**8.** Sew two segments from step 7 together in pairs as shown. Press. Make four.

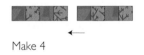

Make 4

**9.** Sew units from step 8 together as shown. Press.

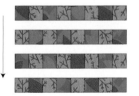

**10.** Sew one 1½" x 6½" Fabric G piece to one remaining segment from step 7 as shown. Press. Make two.

1½

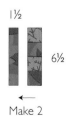

6½

Make 2

**11.** Sew unit from step 9 between two units from step 10 as shown. Press. Sew 2" x 17½" Fabric G piece to bottom of unit as shown. Press.

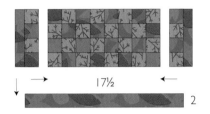

17½

2

**12.** Sew background unit from step 6 to unit from step 11 as shown. Press.

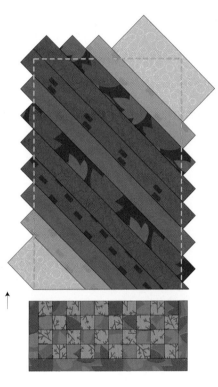

## Adding the Appliqués

Refer to appliqué instructions on page 93. Our instructions are for Quick-Fuse Appliqué, but if you prefer hand appliqué, reverse patterns and add ¼"-wide seam allowances.

**1.** Referring to Quick Fuse Appliqué on page 93, trace patterns for Nest and Bird on page 33 onto on paper side of fusible web. Use assorted scraps to prepare one of each appliqué for fusing.

**2.** Refer to photo and layout on pages 28 and 29 to position and fuse appliqués. Finish appliqué edges with machine satin stitch or other decorative stitches as desired.

**3.** Referring to Couching Technique on page 95, photo and layout on pages 28 and 29, couch assorted yarns and feathers to embellish nest.

**4.** Refer to Embroidery Stitch Guide on page 95. Use three strands of embroidery floss and French knot to make eye on bird.

## Layering and Finishing

**1.** Arrange and baste 23" x 34" backing, batting, and top together, referring to Layering the Quilt on page 94. Hand or machine quilt as desired.

**2.** From back of frame, measure maximum opening including rabbet (groove on back of frame). Cut mounting board slightly smaller (about ⅛") than opening. If frame does not have rabbets, cut mounting board at least ¼" larger than inside dimensions on all sides.

**3.** Temporarily place frame over quilt to determine desired position. Trim excess fabric if desired, leaving approximately two inches on each side to wrap around mounting board. Place quilt on mounting board folding excess fabric to back and secure in place using a needle and thread and a lacing technique like the one illustrated below.

**4.** Place quilt in frame and secure as desired. Add choice of hanger and install on wall.

# Add a Border and Bind It!

*If you prefer to add a border and binding to the wall quilt instead of framing it, follow these steps.*

## Additional Materials Needed

Outside Border - ¼ yard
    Three 2" x 42" strips
Binding - ⅓ yard
    Three 2¾" x 42" strips

## Finishing the Quilt

**1.** Trim quilt top to desired size. The quilt in the layout below was trimmed to 14½" x 25½".

**2.** Refer to Adding the Borders on page 94. Sew 2"-wide Outside Border strips to top, bottom, and sides of quilt. Press.

**3.** Arrange and baste 23" x 34" backing, batting, and quilt top together referring to Layering the Quilt on page 94. Hand or machine quilt as desired.

**4.** Refer to Binding the Quilt on page 95, and using 2¾"-wide binding strips bind quilt to finish. Finished size of this quilt is 18" x 29".

*Finished Size: 18" x 29"*

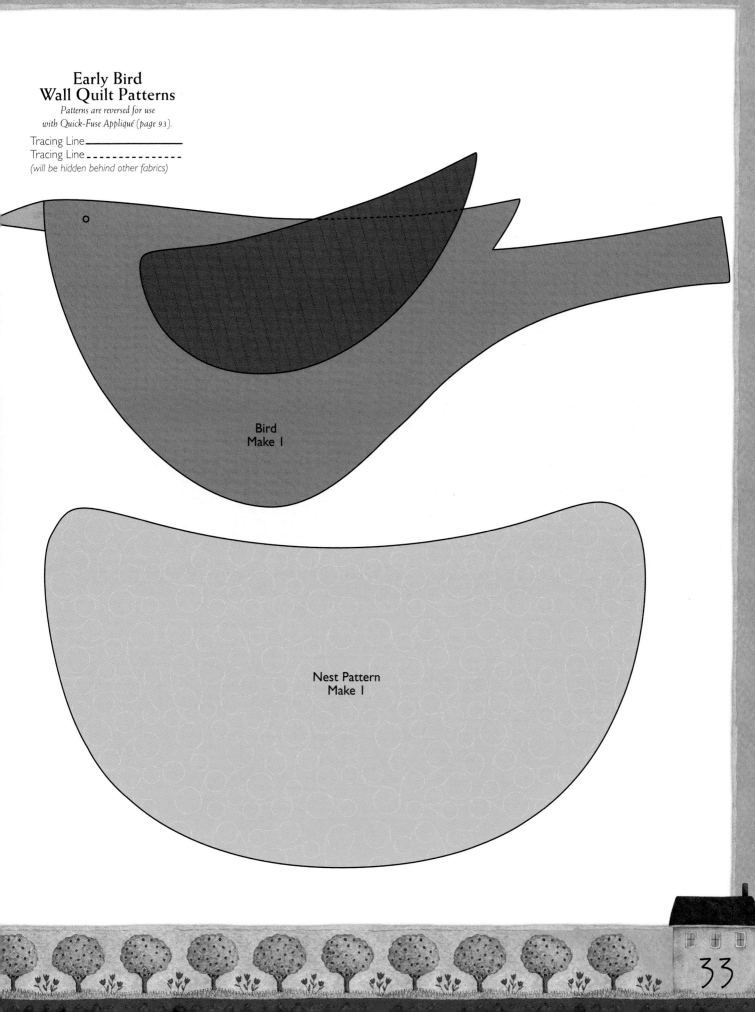

### Early Bird
### Wall Quilt Patterns
*Patterns are reversed for use*
*with Quick-Fuse Appliqué (page 93).*

Tracing Line ————————
Tracing Line - - - - - - - - - - - -
*(will be hidden behind other fabrics)*

Bird
Make 1

Nest Pattern
Make 1

# Summer

Glorious summer
tickles our senses
and invites us
to run and play.

Play the day away with bright, bold
beautiful quilts that are as at home in the
garden as they are on a bed. Lazy daisies
and vibrant pinwheels combine for a
summertime sensation.

# Playful Pinwheels Bed Quilt

Finished Size: 85" x 10

Three times the fun! Pinwheels in three sizes spin in the wind
on this colorful quilt that's the epitome of summer fun.
The bold red, yellow, blue, and crisp white color scheme
has a nautical flair and will make this quilt perfect
for a child's bed or lakeside cottage.

36

# Fabric Requirements and Cutting Instructions

Read all instructions before beginning and use ¼"-wide seam allowances throughout. Read Cutting Strips and Pieces on page 92 prior to cutting fabrics.

| Playful Pinwheels 85" x 102" | FIRST CUT | | SECOND CUT | |
|---|---|---|---|---|
| | Number of Strips or Pieces | Dimensions | Number of Pieces | Dimensions |
| **Fabric A** Pinwheel Background 2⅓ yards | 5 10 10 | 5" x 42" 3" x 42" 2½" x 42" | 40 120 80 | 5" squares 3" squares 2½" x 4½" |
| **Fabric B** Block Background 1¼ yards | 7 | 5⅞" x 42" | 40 | 5⅞" squares |
| **Fabric C** Large Pinwheel ⅝ yard | 4 | 4½" x 42" | 28 | 4½" squares |
| **Fabric D** Large Pinwheel ⅝ yard | 4 | 4½" x 42" | 28 | 4½" squares |
| **Fabric E** Large Pinwheel ½ yard | 3 | 4½" x 42" | 24 | 4½" squares |
| **Fabric F** Medium Pinwheel ½ yard | 3 | 5" x 42" | 20 | 5" squares |
| **Fabric G** Medium Pinwheel ½ yard | 3 | 5" x 42" | 20 | 5" squares |
| **Fabric H** Small Pinwheel ⅔ yard | 4 4 | 3" x 42" 2½" x 42" | 42 28 | 3" squares 2½" x 4½" |
| **Fabric I** Small Pinwheel ⅔ yard | 4 4 | 3" x 42" 2½" x 42" | 42 28 | 3" squares 2½" x 4½" |
| **Fabric J** Small Pinwheel ⅝ yard | 3 3 | 3" x 42" 2½" x 42" | 36 24 | 3" squares 2½" x 4½" |
| **Fabric K** Block Sashing 2⅝ yards | 34 | 2½" x 42" | 80 80 | 2½" x 9⅞" 2½" x 5⅞" |
| **Fabric L** Pinwheel Sashing ⅞ yard | 10 | 2½" x 42" | 80 | 2½" x 4½" |

## Playful Pinwheels Bed Quilt

*Finished Size: 85" x 102"*

| Playful Pinwheels continued | FIRST CUT | |
|---|---|---|
| | Number of Strips or Pieces | Dimensions |
| **BORDERS** | | |
| **First Border** ⅝ yard | 8 | 2½" x 42" |
| **Second Border** ½ yard | 9 | 1½" x 42" |
| **Outside Border** 1½ yards | 9 | 5½" x 42" |
| **Binding** ⅞ yard | 10 | 2¾" x 42" |
| Backing - 7¾ yards Batting - 93" x 110" | | |

## Getting Started

This quilt features three different sizes of pinwheel units in a variety of colors. The large and small pinwheels are set on point and the medium-size pinwheels are incorporated into the sashing. You will be making twenty Pinwheel Blocks measuring 17½" square unfinished. Refer to Accurate Seam Allowance on page 92. Whenever possible, use the Assembly Line Method on page 92. Press seams in the direction of arrows.

## Making the Pinwheel Blocks

**1.** Sew one 2½" x 4½" Fabric A piece to one 2½" x 4½" Fabric H piece. Press. Make twenty-eight.

4½
2½
2½

Make 28

**2.** Refer to Quick Corner Triangles on page 92. Draw a diagonal line on wrong side of units from step 1, noting direction of drawn line to seams. Place one marked unit and one 4½" Fabric C square right sides together. **Sew on drawn line.** Trim ¼" away from stitched line as shown. Press. Make twenty-eight of Unit 1.

**Unit 1**

Unit from step 1
C = 4½" x 4½"
Make 28

←
Make 28
C/AH Fabric

**3.** Repeat steps 1 and 2, using twenty-eight 2½" x 4½" Fabric A pieces, twenty-eight 2½" x 4½" Fabric I pieces and twenty-eight 4½" Fabric D squares to make twenty-eight of Unit 2.

**Unit 2**

←
D/IA Fabrics
Make 28

**4.** Repeat steps 1 and 2, using twenty-four 2½" x 4½" Fabric A pieces, twenty-four 2½" x 4½" Fabric J pieces and twenty-four 4½" Fabric E squares to make twenty-four of Unit 3.

**Unit 3**

←
E/JA Fabrics
Make 24

**5.** Sew units from step 2 together in pairs as shown. Press. Make fourteen.

Make 14

**6.** Sew two units from step 5 together as shown. Press. Make seven Unit 1 Large Pinwheels.

**Unit 1**

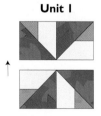

Make 7

**7.** Repeat steps 5 and 6 to make seven Unit 2 Large Pinwheels and six Unit 3 Large Pinwheels.

**Unit 2**        **Unit 3**

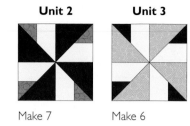

Make 7        Make 6

**8.** To make half-square triangles, draw diagonal line on wrong side of one 3" Fabric A square. Place marked square and one 3" Fabric H square right sides together as shown. Sew a scant ¼" away from drawn line on both sides. Make forty-two. **Cut on drawn line.** Press. Square to 2½". This will make eighty-four Unit 1 half-square triangles.

**Unit 1**

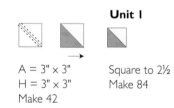

A = 3" x 3"        Square to 2½
H = 3" x 3"        Make 84
Make 42

**9.** Repeat step 8 using forty-two 3" Fabric A squares and forty-two 3" Fabric I squares to make eighty-four Unit 2 half-square triangles.

**Unit 2**

→
I/A Fabrics
Square to 2½
Make 84

**10.** Repeat step 8 using thirty-six 3" Fabric A squares and thirty-six 3" Fabric J squares to make seventy-two Unit 3 half-square triangle units.

**Unit 3**

→
J/A Fabrics
Square to 2½
Make 72

**11** Sew one 2½" x 4½" Fabric L piece between two units from step 8, noting orientation of units as shown. Press. Make twenty-eight.

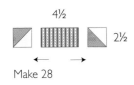

4½

2½

Make 28

**12.** Sew one unit from step 11 between two units from step 8, noting orientation of units as shown. Press. Make fourteen.

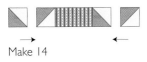

Make 14

**13.** Repeat steps 11 and 12 using twenty-eight 2½" x 4½" Fabric L pieces and units from step 9, noting orientation of units before sewing. Make number of units shown.

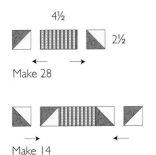

4½

2½

Make 28

Make 14

**14.** Repeat steps 11 and 12 using twenty-four 2½" x 4½" Fabric L pieces and units from step 10, noting orientation of units before sewing. Make number of units shown.

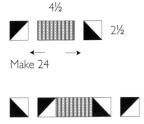

4½

2½

Make 24

Make 12

**15.** Sew one unit from step 6 between two units from step 11. Press. Make seven.

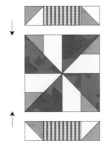

Make 7

**16.** Sew one unit from step 15 between two units from step 12. Press. Make seven Unit 1 Pinwheels.

**Unit 1**

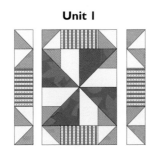

Make 7

**17.** Repeat steps 15 and 16, using Unit 2 from steps 7 and 13 to make seven Unit 2 Pinwheels. Repeat steps 15 and 16, using Unit 3 from steps 7 and 14 to make six Unit 3 Pinwheels.

**Unit 2**

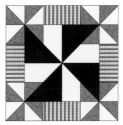

Make 7

**Unit 3**

Make 6

**18.** Sew one 5⅞" Fabric B square between two 2½" x 5⅞" Fabric K pieces as shown. Press. Sew this unit between two 2½" x 9⅞" Fabric K pieces. Press. Make forty.

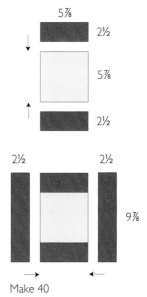

5⅞

2½

5⅞

2½

2½          2½

9⅞

Make 40

**19.** Draw a diagonal line on wrong side of one unit from step 18 as shown. Stay-stitch (use 4 mm stitch length) ⅛" away from drawn line on both sides. This will prevent stretching when sewing to pinwheel units. Cut on drawn line to make eighty Corner Triangle units.

Stay Stitch Line
Cutting Line
Stay Stitch Line

Make 80 Corner Triangle Units

**20.** Fold corner triangles and blocks to find midpoints. Matching midpoints, sew one Unit 1 Pinwheel from step 16 between two Corner Triangles from step 19 as shown. Press. Sew two Corner Triangles to remaining sides as shown. Press. Make seven. Square to 17½".

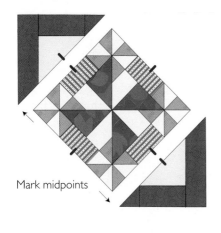

Mark midpoints

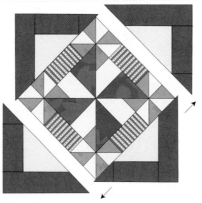

Make 7
Square to 17½"

**21.** Repeat step 20, using Unit 2 Pinwheels from step 17 and Corner Triangles from step 19 to make seven blocks. Repeat step 20, using Unit 3 Pinwheels from step 17 and Corner Triangles to make six blocks.

Make 7
Square to 17½"

Make 6
Square to 17½"

**22.** Making half-square triangles, draw diagonal line on wrong side of twenty 5" Fabric A squares. Place one marked square and one 5" Fabric F square right sides together. Sew a scant ¼" away from drawn line on both sides. Make twenty. Cut on drawn line. Press. Square to 4½". This will make forty Unit 4 half-square triangles.

**Unit 4**

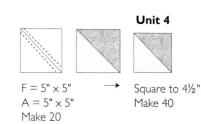

F = 5" × 5"      Square to 4½"
A = 5" × 5"      Make 40
Make 20

**23.** Making half-square triangles, draw diagonal line on wrong side of twenty 5" Fabric A squares. Place one marked square and one 5" Fabric G square right sides together as shown. Sew a scant ¼" away from drawn line on both sides. Make twenty. Cut on drawn line. Press. Square to 4½". This will make forty Unit 5 half-square triangles.

**Unit 5**

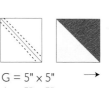

G = 5" × 5"      Square to 4½"
A = 5" × 5"      Make 40
Make 20

**24.** Making Quick Corner Triangles, sew two Unit 4 half-square triangles and two Unit 5 half-square triangles to one Unit 1 Pinwheel from step 20 as shown. Press. Make seven Block 1 Pinwheels. Blocks measure 17½" square.

**Block 1**

←          ←
Make 7
Block measures 17½" square

**25.** Repeat step 24 to sew two Unit 4 and two Unit 5 half-square triangles to each Unit 2 and 3 Pinwheels from step 21. Make seven Block 2 Pinwheels and six Block 3 Pinwheels. Blocks measure 17½" square.

**Block 2**                       **Block 3**

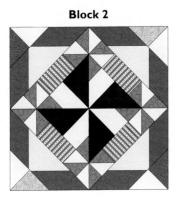 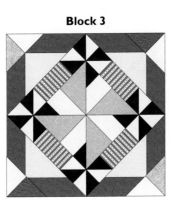

Make 7                             Make 6
Blocks measure 17½" square           Blocks measure 17½" square

## Assembly

**1.** Referring to photo and layout on pages 36 and 37, sew together two Block 1 Pinwheels, one Block 2 Pinwheel, and one Block 3 Pinwheel noting orientation of corner triangle units as shown. Press seams open. Make two and label Rows 1 and 4.

**2.** Referring to photo and layout on pages 36 and 37, sew together two Block 2 Pinwheels, one Block 3 Pinwheel, and one Block 1 Pinwheel noting orientation of corner triangle units as shown. Press seams open. Make two and label Rows 2 and 5.

**3.** Referring to photo and layout on pages 36 and 37, sew together two Block 3 Pinwheels, one Block 1 Pinwheel, and one Block 2 Pinwheel noting orientation of corner triangle units as shown. Press seams open. Label Row 3.

**4.** Referring to photo and layout on pages 36 and 37, sew rows together. Press.

## Adding the Borders

**1.** Sew 2½" x 42" First Border strips end-to-end to make one continuous 2½"-wide strip. Press. Referring to Adding the Borders on page 94, measure quilt through center from side to side. Cut two 2½"-wide First Border strips to that measurement. Sew to top and bottom of quilt. Press seams toward border.

**2.** Measure quilt through center from top to bottom, including borders just added. Cut two 2½"-wide First Border strips to that measurement. Sew to sides of quilt. Press.

**3.** Referring to steps 1 and 2, join, measure, trim, and sew 1½"-wide Second Border strips and 5½"-wide Outside Border strips to top, bottom, and sides of quilt. Press seams toward each newly added border.

## Finishing the Quilt

**1.** Cut backing crosswise into three equal pieces. Sew pieces together to make one 93" x 120" (approximate) backing piece. Press.

**2.** Arrange and baste backing, batting, and top together, referring to Layering the Quilt on page 94. Hand or machine quilt as desired.

**3.** Sew 2¾" x 42" binding strips end-to-end to make one continuous 2¾"-wide strip. Press. Refer to Binding the Quilt on page 95 and bind quilt to finish.

# Daisy Daze Lap Quilt

Finished Size: 61½" x 61¼

You'll be dazed and amazed at the way a few simple seams create such an interesting pattern when you use a striped fabric to make your blocks. Sunshine-bright daisies on easily pieced background squares alternate with the striped blocks to make a quilt that is as dazzling as it is delightful.

## Fabric Requirements and Cutting Instructions

Read all instructions before beginning and use ¼"-wide seam allowances throughout. Read Cutting Strips and Pieces on page 92 prior to cutting fabrics.

| Daisy Daze Lap Quilt 61½" x 61½" | FIRST CUT | | SECOND CUT | |
|---|---|---|---|---|
| | Number of Strips or Pieces | Dimensions | Number of Pieces | Dimensions |
| **Fabric A** Flower Background ⅔ yard | 2 | 11" x 42" | 6 | 11" squares |
| **Fabric B** Flower Background ⅔ yard | 2 | 11" x 42" | 6 | 11" squares |
| **Fabric C** Maze Blocks 2 yards* | 6 1 | 58" x 6½"* 13" x 42"* | | |
| | | *Twelve blocks are cut from 58" x 6½" strips, the thirteenth block is cut from 13" x 42" strip.* | | |
| **BORDERS** | | | | |
| **First Border** ¼ yard | 5 | 1½" x 42" | | |
| **Second Border** ⅜ yard | 6 | 2" x 42" | | |
| **Third Border** ⅓ yard | 6 | 1½" x 42" | | |
| **Outside Border** ⅔ yard | 6 | 3½" x 42" | | |
| **Binding** ⅝ yard | 7 | 2¾" x 42" | | |

Backing - 4 yards
Batting - 69" x 69"
Flower Petal Appliqués - ⅙ yard **each** of four fabrics
Flower Center Appliqués - ⅛ yard
Lightweight Fusible Web - 1¾ yards
Template Plastic

*For directional fabric, the size that is listed first runs parallel to selvage.*

## Daisy Daze Lap Quilt

*Finished Size: 61½" x 61½"*

## Getting Started

The daisies seem to dance across this quilt with the play of alternating Daisy and Maze Blocks. Each block measures 10" unfinished. The daisies are quick-fused and edges are finished with decorative stitching. Whenever possible, use the Assembly Line Method on page 92. Press seams in the direction of arrows.

## Making the Daisy Block

Refer to appliqué instructions on page 93. Our instructions are for Quick-Fuse appliqué, but if you prefer hand appliqué, add ¼" seam allowances.

**1.** Draw a diagonal line on wrong side of one 11" Fabric B square. Place marked square and one 11" Fabric A square right sides together. Sew a scant ¼" away from drawn line on both sides to make half-square triangle. Make six. Cut on drawn line. Press seam open. This will make twelve half-square triangles.

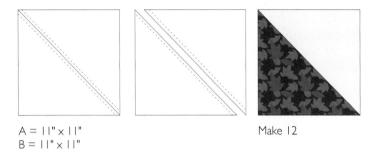

A = 11" x 11"
B = 11" x 11"
Make 6

Make 12

**2.** Draw a diagonal line on wrong side of one unit from step 1 in opposite direction from seam as shown. Place marked unit and one unmarked unit from step 1, right sides together, matching seams and placing Fabric A triangle on top of Fabric B triangle. Sew a scant ¼" away from drawn line on both sides. Make six. Cut on drawn line and press seams open. Square to 10". This will make twelve quarter-square triangle units.

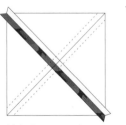

Unit from step 1
Make 6

Square to 10"
Make 12

**3.** Refer to Quick-Fuse Appliqué on page 93. Using flower pattern on page 46, trace seventy-two petals and twelve centers on paper side of fusible web. Using Flower Petal Fabrics make eighteen petals for each fabric. Using Flower Center Fabric prepare appliqués for fusing. Arrange and fuse flower pieces to blocks as desired. Finish appliqué edges with machine satin stitch or other decorative stitching as desired. Flower Block measures 10" square.

Make 6

Make 6
Block measures 10" square

## Making the Maze Blocks

**1.** Referring to triangle pattern on page 47, draw pattern on template plastic or heavy card stock. Cut out template and trace four triangles on 58" x 6½" Fabric C strip, aligning bottom edge with stripe, as shown. This will make one Maze square. Invert pattern and drawn another set of triangles, aligning bottom edge with stripe. Repeat to make a total of fifty-two triangles or thirteen sets of four matching triangles.

*Note: Twelve blocks can be cut from six 58" x 6½" strips. Use 13" x 42" strip to cut four matching striped pieces for the last block.*

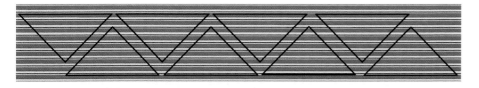

**2.** Sew matching triangles from step 1 together in pairs. Press seams open. Sew two matching pairs of triangles together to make Maze Block. Press. Make thirteen. Block measures 10" square.

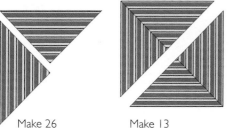

Make 26

Make 13
Block measures 10" square

## Assembly

**1.** Referring to photo and layout on pages 42 and 43, arrange and sew together three Maze Blocks and two Flower Blocks to make row noting orientation of flower blocks. Press seams toward Maze Blocks. Make three.

**2.** Referring to photo and layout on pages 42 and 43, arrange and sew together three Flower Blocks and two Maze Blocks to make row noting orientation of flower blocks. Press seams toward Maze Blocks. Make two.

**3.** Referring to photo and layout on pages 42 and 43, arrange and sew together rows from steps 1 and 2. Press.

**4.** Sew 1½" x 42" First Border strips end-to-end to make one continuous 1½"-wide strip. Press. Referring to Adding the Borders on page 94, measure quilt through center from side to side. Cut two 1½"-wide First Border strips to that measurement. Sew to top and bottom of quilt. Press seams toward border.

**5.** Measure quilt through center from top to bottom, including borders just added. Cut two 1½"-wide First Border strips to that measurement. Sew to sides of quilt. Press.

**6.** Referring to steps 4 and 5, join, measure, trim and sew 2"-wide Second Border, 1½"-wide Third Border, and 3½"-wide Outside Border strips to top, bottom and sides of quilt. Press seams toward each newly added border.

## Finishing the Quilt

**1.** Cut backing crosswise into two equal pieces. Sew pieces together to make one 72" x 80" (approximate) backing piece. Press.

**2.** Arrange and baste backing, batting, and top together, referring to Layering the Quilt on page 94. Hand or machine quilt as desired.

**3.** Sew 2¾" x 42" binding strips end-to-end to make one continuous 2¾"-wide strip. Refer to Binding the Quilt on page 95 and bind quilt to finish.

## Daisy Daze
## Lap Quilt Patterns

Tracing Line ———————
Tracing Line - - - - - - - - - -
*(will be hidden behind other fabrics)*

Maze Block Pattern

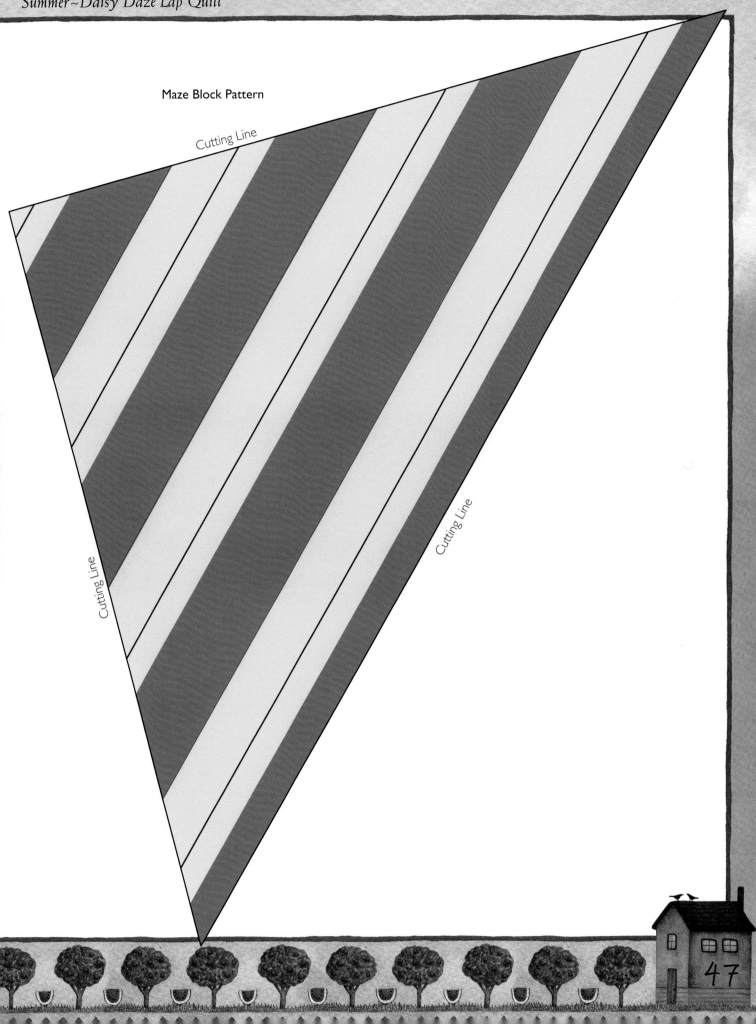

Cutting Line

Cutting Line

Cutting Line

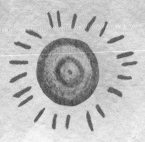

# Daisy Daze Pillow

**Quick!**

Finished Size: 21½" x 21½

*She loves me, she loves me a lot....you won't be pulling any petals from this cute daisy as it is perfect just the way it is. You'll love our easy construction technique and the vibrant simplicity of this go-everywhere pillow.*

# Fabric Requirements and Cutting Instructions

Read all instructions before beginning and use ¼"-wide seam allowances throughout. Read Cutting Strips and Pieces on page 92 prior to cutting fabrics.

| Daisy Daze Pillow 21½" x 21½" | FIRST CUT | | SECOND CUT | |
|---|---|---|---|---|
| | Number of Strips or Pieces | Dimensions | Number of Pieces | Dimensions |
| ☐ **Fabric A** Center and Lining ⅔ yard | 1 1 | 24" square (*lining*) 10" square | | |
| ▨ **Fabric B** First Border ⅛ yard | 2 | 1½" x 42" | 2 2 | 1½" x 12" 1½" x 10" |
| ■ **Fabric C** Second Border ¼ yard | 2 | 2½" x 42" | 2 2 | 2½" x 16" 2½" x 12" |
| ▤ **Fabric D** Outside Triangles & Backing 1½ yards | 1 3 | 22" x 42" 9½" x 42" | 2 2 2 | 22" x 14" 9½" x 34" 9½" x 16" |

**Flower Appliqués** - Assorted scraps
**Lightweight Fusible Web** - ⅓ yard
**Fiberfill**
**Pillow Form Fabric** - 1¼ yards (two 22" squares)

## Daisy Daze Pillow

*Finished Size: 21½" x 21½"*

# Making the Pillow

**1.** Sew 10" Fabric A square between two 1½" x 10" Fabric B pieces. Press seams toward Fabric B. Sew this unit between two 1½" x 12" Fabric B pieces. Press.

**2.** Sew unit from step 1 between two 2½" x 12" Fabric C pieces. Press seams toward Fabric C. Sew this unit between two 2½" x 16" Fabric C pieces. Press.

**3.** Sew unit from step 2 between two 9½" x 16" Fabric D pieces. Press seams toward Fabric D. Sew this unit between two 9½" x 34" Fabric D pieces. Press.

**4.** Referring to diagram, square unit, from step 3, to 22", allowing for ¼"-wide seam allowance at points.

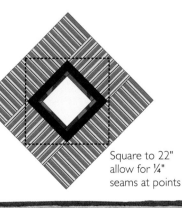

Square to 22" allow for ¼" seams at points

**5.** Refer to Quick-Fuse Appliqué on page 93, flower pattern on page 46, and layout, and use appliqué flower scraps to appliqué six petals and one flower center to pillow. Finish all appliqué edges with satin stitch or decorative stitching as desired.

**6.** Refer to Finishing the Pillows, step 1, on page 95 to prepare pillow top for quilting. Quilt as desired.

**7.** Use two 22" x 14" Fabric D backing pieces and refer to Finishing the Pillows, page 95, steps 2-4 to sew backing. Refer to Pillow Forms on page 95 to make 21½" pillow form.

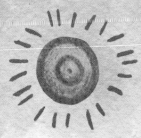

# Sunshine Cooler

Set the scene for outdoor living with this fun cooler that's right at home at a picnic or on the patio. The sunny daisy center is topped (appropriately!) with a red bottle cap for a touch of whimsy. A "resist" method makes the daisy and stripes as simple as they are stunning.

APPLES

## Materials Needed

Galvanized Tin Washtub or
  Beverage Holder
Household Vinegar
Light Gray Spray Metal Primer
Acrylic Craft Paints -
  **Americana®:** Moon Yellow,
  Golden Straw
  **Delta Ceramcoat®:** Cardinal
  Red, Denim Blue, Nightfall,
  Midnight Blue
Sea Sponge & Assorted Paintbrushes
Scotch® Magic™ Tape
1½" wide Scotch® Safe-Release™
  Painters' Masking Tape
Metal Bottle Cap
Hot Glue Gun
Spray Matte Varnish
Template Plastic
Disposable Plate or Paper Palette
Craft Knife
Sandpaper

## Painting the Beverage Cooler

**1.** Wash unfinished galvanized tin beverage holder or washtub with vinegar, scrubbing well, then rinse thoroughly and allow to dry. This treatment removes the oils used in manufacturing tin products. (If beverage holder has been previously painted, sand well to remove all gloss and wash in vinegar as described above.) When thoroughly dry, spray tin and bottle cap with metal primer. Allow to dry.

**2.** Referring to photo, paint approximately 1" around the rim and a 10" square in the front center of the tin with Moon Yellow paint. Two coats may be necessary for good coverage.

**3.** Dampen sea sponge with water and wring thoroughly. Place small amounts of Moon Yellow paint and Golden Straw paint on a disposable plate or paper palette. Dip sea sponge in each color and blot paint by tapping on a paper towel several times. Using a tapping motion, sponge paint onto yellow square. Use a light touch to achieve a stippled effect. Refill sponge as necessary, and adjust amount of each color on the sponge to achieve desired effect. Allow to dry.

**4.** Using petal pattern on page 46, trace one petal onto template plastic. Using plastic template, cut six petals out of the Painters' Masking Tape, handling carefully. Place tape petals on yellow square, spacing evenly as shown in photo. Run finger over edges of each petal to increase adhesion. Use Scotch® Magic™ Tape to mask off a ½"-wide stripe at the top of tin. Run finger over the edge to increase adhesion.

*Note: you can use masking tape for this purpose, but we find that there is less bleed through with Scotch® Magic™ Tape so you get a crisper line. For best results, use the Scotch® Magic™ brand name only.*

**5.** With masks in place and using a soft brush, paint entire tin Denim Blue, being very careful when painting over petal areas. Allow Denim Blue paint to dry. Referring to step 3, sponge area with Denim Blue and Nightfall paint making area around petals a little darker than rest of the container. When paint is thoroughly dry, remove the masking tape. A craft knife may be needed to lift an edge of the tape to get it started. A softer look is preferred for this project, so if edges aren't crisp on the petals, don't worry. Lightly sand over the petals to remove high points and blend edges. Remove Scotch® Magic™ Tape to expose yellow rim.

**6.** Referring to photo and using Scotch® Magic™ Tape to mask areas, add a Midnight Blue stripe on the bottom and thin Cardinal Red and Midnight Blue stripes close to top. Paint bottom rim of container Cardinal Red and handles Midnight Blue.

**7.** Paint bottle cap Cardinal Red, allow to dry, and use a large glob of hot glue to affix it to the center of the flower.

**8.** Apply several coats of matte varnish to the container.

*Note: We recommend that the inside of the container not be painted if you plan to use it to hold ice. Water will damage the paint over time. If you choose to paint the inside of your cooler, line cooler with a clear plastic sack before filling with ice.*

51

# Autumn

Autumn's bounty
is a feast
for the eyes
as well as
the palate.

Enjoy the splendor of fall's spicy hues,
both inside and out, with quilts made
for snuggling and a rustic runner and
bountiful bowl for the table.

# Autumn Spice Lap Quilt

**Quick!**

Finished Size: 53" x 5?

Curry, cayenne, and paprika are the harvest hues that
spice up this piquant quilt that's seasoned with simple oak leaves.
A modified log cabin technique is accented with sashing and
a variety of borders for a quilt that's as visually appealing
as it is quick and easy.

# Fabric Requirements and Cutting Instructions

Read all instructions before beginning and use ¼"-wide seam allowances throughout. Read Cutting Strips and Pieces on page 92 prior to cutting fabrics.

## Autumn Spice Lap Quilt

*Finished Size: 53" x 57"*

| Autumn Spice Lap Quilt 53" x 57" | FIRST CUT | | SECOND CUT | |
|---|---|---|---|---|
| | Number of Strips or Pieces | Dimensions | Number of Pieces | Dimensions |
| **Fabric A** Block Center ¼ yard | 1 | 5½" x 42" | 4 | 5½" x 7½" |
| **Fabric B** First Log Strip ⅙ yard | 2 | 2" x 42" | 4 4 | 2" x 10½" 2" x 5½" |
| **Fabric C** First Log Strip ⅙ yard | 2 | 2" x 42" | 4 4 | 2" x 10½" 2" x 5½" |
| **Fabric D** Second Log Strip & Sashing ½ yard | 3 4 | 2" x 42" 1½" x 42" *(sashing)* | 4 4 4 4 | 2" x 13½" 2" x 8½" 1½" x 20½" 1½" x 18½" |
| **Fabric E** Second Log Strip ¼ yard | 3 | 2" x 42" | 4 4 | 2" x 13½" 2" x 8½" |
| **Fabric F** Third Log Strip ⅓ yard | 4 | 2" x 42" | 4 4 | 2" x 16½" 2" x 11½" |
| **Fabric G** Third Log Strip ⅓ yard | 4 | 2" x 42" | 4 4 | 2" x 16½" 2" x 11½" |
| **Fabric H** Fourth Log Strip ⅓ yard | 4 | 2½" x 42" | 4 4 | 2½" x 20½" 2½" x 14½" |
| **Fabric I** Fourth Log Strip ⅓ yard | 4 | 2½" x 42" | 4 4 | 2½" x 20½" 2½" x 14½" |
| **Fabric J** Sashing ⅛ yard | 2 | 1½" x 42" | 2 2 | 1½" x 20½" 1½" x 18½" |
| **Fabric K** Center Square Scrap | 1 | 3½" square | | |

Backing - 3⅓ yards
Batting - 59" x 63"
Leaf Appliqués - Assorted wool scraps
Lightweight Fusible Web - ⅓ yard

| Autumn Spice Lap Quilt Continued | FIRST CUT | |
|---|---|---|
| | Number of Strips or Pieces | Dimensions |
| **BORDERS** | | |
| **First Border** ¼ yard | 5 | 1½" x 42" |
| **Second Border** ⅓ yard | 5 | 2" x 42" |
| **Third Border** ¼ yard | 5 | 1½" x 42" |
| **Outside Border** ⅔ yard | 6 | 3½" x 42" |
| **Binding** ⅝ yard | 6 | 2¾" x 42" |

## Getting Started

This simple quilt is a breeze to make. The quilt consists of four blocks based on the Courthouse Step design and features a wool leaf appliqué in the center of each block. Refer to Accurate Seam Allowance on page 92. Whenever possible use the Assembly Line Method on page 92. Press seams in direction of arrows.

## Making the Block

1. Sew one 5½" x 7½" Fabric A piece between one 2" x 5½" Fabric B piece and one 2" x 5½" Fabric C piece as shown. Press. Make four.

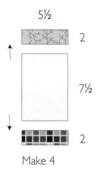

5½
2
7½
2
Make 4

2. Sew unit from step 1 between one 2" x 10½" Fabric C piece and one 2" x 10½" Fabric B piece as shown. Press. Make four.

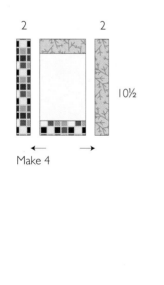

2
2
10½
Make 4

3. Sew unit from step 2 between one 2" x 8½" Fabric D piece and one 2" x 8½" Fabric E piece as shown. Press. Sew this unit between one 2" x 13½" Fabric E piece and one 2" x 13½" Fabric D piece. Press. Make four.

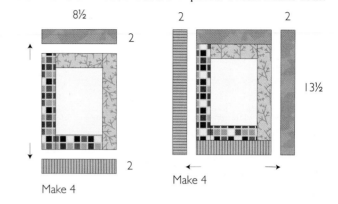

8½
2
2
2
13½
Make 4
Make 4

4. Sew unit from step 3 between one 2" x 11½" Fabric F piece and one 2" x 11½" Fabric G piece as shown. Press. Sew this unit between one 2" x 16½" Fabric G strip and one 2" x 16½" Fabric F strip. Press. Make four.

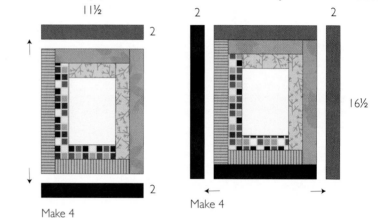

11½
2
2
2
16½
Make 4
Make 4

5. Sew unit from step 4 between one 2½" x 14½" Fabric H strip and one 2½" x 14½" Fabric I strip as shown. Press. Sew this unit between one 2½" x 20½" Fabric I strip and one 2½" x 20½" Fabric H strip. Press. Make four. Block measures 18½" x 20½".

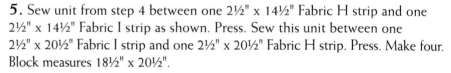
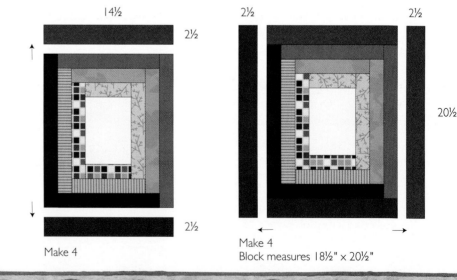

14½
2½
2½
2½
20½
2½
Make 4
Make 4
Block measures 18½" x 20½"

56

**6.** Sew 1½" x 18½" Fabric J strip between two 1½" x 18½" Fabric D strips as shown. Press. Make two.

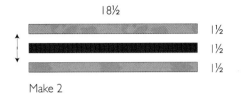

Make 2

**7.** Referring to photo and layout on pages 54 and 55, sew one unit from step 6 between two units from step 5. Press. Make two.

**8.** Sew 1½" x 20½" Fabric J strip between two 1½" x 20½" Fabric D strips. Press. Make two.

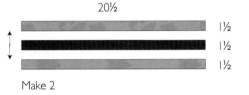

Make 2

**9.** Sew 3½" Fabric K square between two units from step 8 as shown. Press.

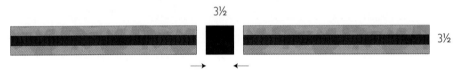

**10.** Referring to photo and layout on pages 54 and 55, sew unit from step 9 between two units from step 7. Press.

## Adding the Appliqués

Refer to appliqué instructions on page 93. Our instructions are for Quick Fuse Appliqué, but if you prefer to use cotton fabric and hand appliqué, add ¼"-wide seam allowances.

**1.** Refer to Quick-Fuse Appliqué on page 93 and Oak Pattern on page 62. Trace four leaves onto paper side of fusible web. Use wool scraps to prepare appliqués for fusing.

**2.** Refer to photo and layout on page 54 and 55. Position and fuse appliqués to quilt. Finish appliqué edges with a machine blanket stitch or other decorative stitching as desired.

## Adding the Borders

**1.** Sew 1½" x 42" First Border strips end-to-end to make one continuous 1½"-wide strip. Press. Referring to Adding the Borders on page 94, measure quilt through center from side to side. Cut two 1½"-wide First Border strips to that measurement. Sew to top and bottom of quilt. Press seams toward border.

**2.** Measure quilt through center from top to bottom, including borders just added. Cut two 1½"-wide First Border strips to that measurement. Sew to sides of quilt. Press.

**3.** Refer to steps 1 and 2 to join, measure, trim, and sew 2"-wide Second Border strips, 1½"-wide Third Border strips, and 3½"-wide Outside Border strips to top, bottom, and sides of quilt. Press seams toward each newly added border.

## Finishing the Quilt

**1.** Cut backing crosswise into two equal pieces. Sew pieces together to make one 59" x 80" (approximate) backing piece. Press and trim to 59" x 63".

**2.** Arrange and baste backing, batting, and top together, referring to Layering the Quilt on page 94. Hand or machine quilt as desired.

**3.** Sew 2¾" x 42" binding strips end-to-end to make one continuous 2¾"-wide strip. Refer to Binding the Quilt on page 95 and bind quilt to finish.

# Autumn Leaves
## Table Runner

Finished Size: 15½" x 5

A pile of leaves, patches, and techniques make this wool table runner a sampler of fall's many savors. The rich colors and textures of wool are accented with a variety of hand and machine embroidery techniques providing a rustic simplicity to this warm and welcoming runner.

## Fabric Requirements and Cutting Instructions

WoolFelt® is used extensively in this table runner. WoolFelt is manufactured by National Nonwovens and is available at many quilt shops and fabric stores. Call (800) 333-3469 for sources. Read all instructions before beginning.

## Materials Needed

**Use wool or WoolFelt® for entire project**

Fabric A (Table Runner) - 1½ yards
   One 14" x 48" piece
Fabric B (Large Appliquéd Patches) - Assorted scraps
   Two 6" squares
   Two 5" x 6" pieces
   Two 4" x 7" pieces
   Two 3" squares
Fabric C (Couched and Embroidered Patches) - Assorted scraps
   Two 4" x 6" pieces
   Two 4" squares
Fabric D (Table Runner Backing) - 1½ yards
   One 18" x 52" piece
Leaf Appliqués - Assorted scraps
Fibers - Assorted yarns, Perle cotton, and embroidery floss
Fabric Stabilizer - 1 yard
Crewel Needle
Assorted Beads (optional)
Wax Pencil

## Autumn Leaves Table Runner

*Finished Size:*
*15½" x 51"*

## Getting Started

Wools give warmth and texture to this table runner. When using felt or felted wool, there is no need to add seam allowances or turn under edges. A variety of patches are attached to the table runner with hand stitching. Leaf appliqués are attached to patches with a machine blanket stitch and leaf outlines are made with yarn that is couched or sewn with a running stitch. Refer to tip box (page 61) for instructions on felting wool and treating WoolFelt® to obtain a Sherpa-like texture. Felt is also available in acrylic fiber, but will not change texture when heated or washed. The table runner is finished using an assortment of yarns to attach the patches. The same yarns are used to make the tassels.

## Making the Table Runner

**1.** Using wax pencil, mark center of each end of 14" x 48" table runner fabric and 7" from edge as shown. Align a ruler at one marked 7" point and marked center point, draw a line connecting points. Using a rotary ruler and cutter, cut off one corner. Repeat for other side and opposite end of runner.

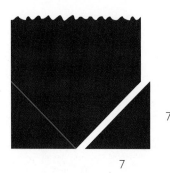

**2.** Referring to Leaf Appliqué patterns on pages 62-63, make templates for White Oak, Oak, Maple, and Alder leaves. Cut number of wool appliqués indicated on pattern.

**3.** Refer to photo and layout on pages 58 and 59 and Machine Appliqué, steps 2-5, on page 93. Attach leaves to Fabric B Patches with a machine blanket stitch or as desired. Attach Maple leaves to 6" x 6" patches; White Oak to 5" x 6" patches; Oak to 4" x 7" patches; and Alder to 3" x 3" patches.

**4.** Refer to Elm and Sycamore Patterns on pages 62 and 63 and Couching Technique and Embroidery Stitch Guide on page 95. Using wax pencil, trace Elm Pattern on two 4" x 6" Fabric C pieces and Sycamore Pattern on two 4" Fabric C squares. Using yarns and a couching technique, follow traced lines to create two sycamore leaf patches and one elm leaf patch. Use yarn and a running stitch to hand-stitch the second elm leaf patch.

**5.** Referring to photo on page 58 and diagram, position and pin Patches to Table Runner as shown.

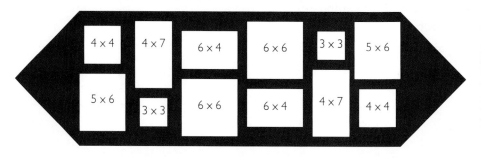

**6.** Referring to Embroidery Stitch Guide on page 95, use a large crewel needle and Perle cotton, embroidery floss, or yarn to stitch Patches to Table Runner. Use a running stitch or primitive stitch.

**7.** Arrange and pin Table Runner on 18" x 52" Fabric D piece.

**8.** Referring to Embroidery Stitch Guide on page 95, use a crewel needle, yarn, and a running stitch to sew Table Runner and Fabric D together. Using a ruler and rotary cutter, trim Fabric D to extend ¾" beyond Table Runner edges on all sides.

## Making the Tassels

**1.** Select a variety of fibers for the tassels. We used eight. Wrap fibers around a 4" ruler or square of cardboard until the desired amount of fullness is obtained. Our fibers were wrapped seven times. Tie 15" piece of Perle cotton around top section of loops as shown and slide fibers off ruler or cardboard. Make two.

**3.** Embellish tassel with beads. Using needle and heavy thread, sew through and around assorted beads, leaving approximately ½" between beads. Referring to photo, wrap beaded thread around tassel and stitch to secure. Make two. Sew one tassel to each pointed end of Table Runner.

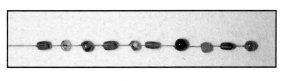

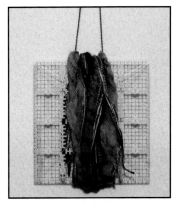

**2.** Wrap 30" piece of Perle cotton thread ½" below loop and tie in place. Continue wrapping the extra length of thread around until a 4"-length remains. Tie securely in place. Cut bottom section of loops and thread to make tassel. Trim fibers as needed for desired length. Make two.

### ~Tip~

A combination of WoolFelt® and wool fabric was used for the table runner. To add a sherpa-like texture to WoolFelt, wet thoroughly with warm water, blot with cotton towel, and place both towel and wool in hot dryer until dry. WoolFelt is manufactured by National Nonwovens and is available at many quilt shops and fabric stores. Call (800) 333-3469 for sources. Felt is also available in acrylic fiber, but will not change texture when heated or washed.

To felt wool fabric, plunge in boiling water for five minutes, then plunge in icy water until very chilled. Do not mix colors as dyes may run. Blot with cotton towel and place both towel and wool in hot dryer until dry.

Remember: most wool will shrink 10-15% when subjected to heat, so additional yardage may be needed.

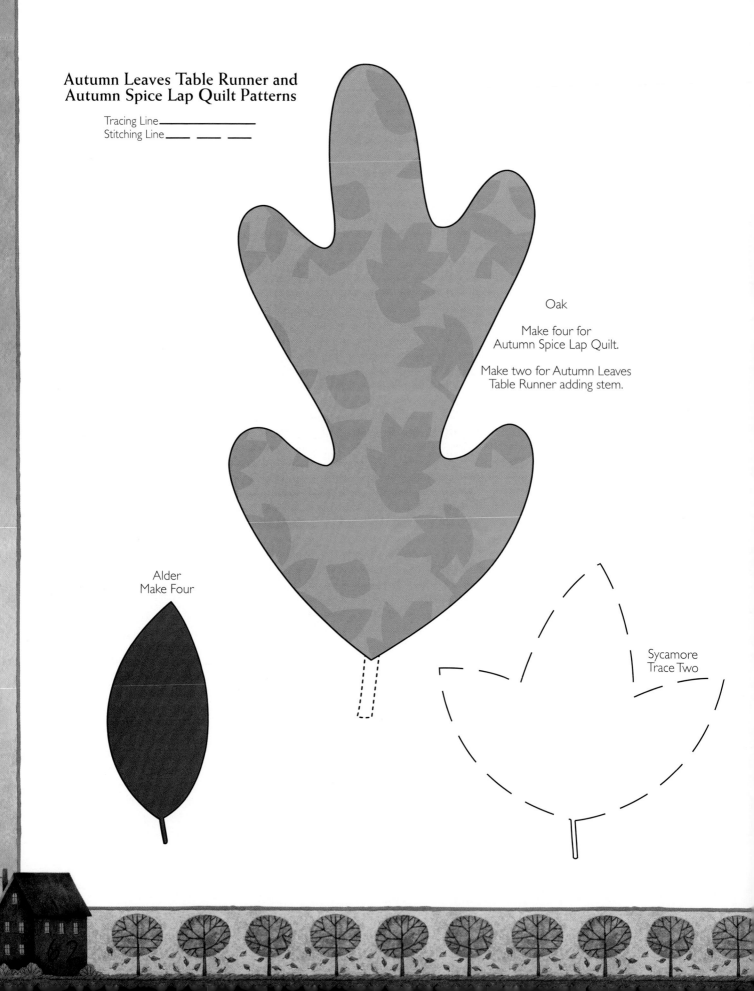

**Autumn Leaves Table Runner and
Autumn Spice Lap Quilt Patterns**

Tracing Line——————
Stitching Line—— —— ——

Oak

Make four for
Autumn Spice Lap Quilt.

Make two for Autumn Leaves
Table Runner adding stem.

Alder
Make Four

Sycamore
Trace Two

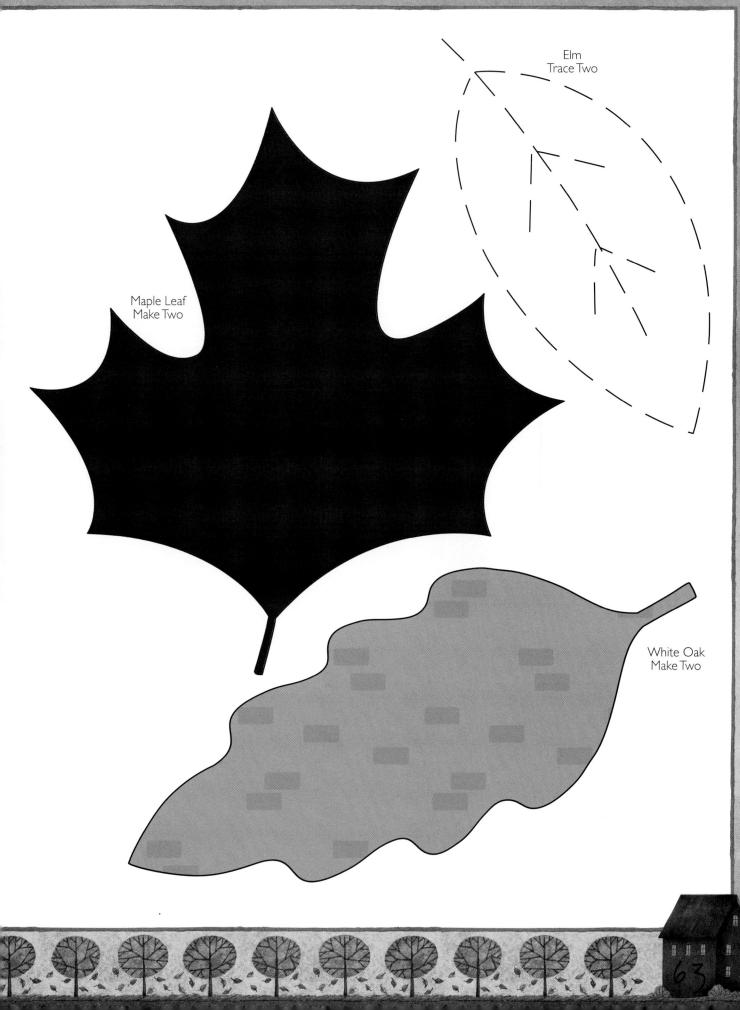

Elm
Trace Two

Maple Leaf
Make Two

White Oak
Make Two

# Bountiful Harvest Quilt

Finished Size: 48″ x 6

As colorful and beautiful as an arboretum in October, this quilt
will remind you of the glories of autumn and the bounty of the
harvest season. Easy quarter-square triangles are the
building blocks for this sensational quilt.

APPLES

# Fabric Requirements and Cutting Instructions

Read all instructions before beginning and use ¼"-wide seam allowances throughout. Read Cutting Strips and Pieces on page 92 prior to cutting fabrics.

## Bountiful Harvest Quilt

*Finished Size: 48" x 60"*

| Bountiful Harvest Quilt 48" x 60" | | FIRST CUT | |
|---|---|---|---|
| | | Number of Strips or Pieces | Dimensions |
| A | **Block 1** ¼ yard **each** of four fabrics | 3* | 8" squares |
| B | | | *Cut for each fabric* |
| C | | | |
| D | | | |
| A | **Block 2** ¼ yard **each** of four fabrics | 3* | 8" squares |
| B | | | *Cut for each fabric* |
| C | | | |
| D | | | |
| A | **Block 3** ¼ yard **each** of four fabrics | 3* | 8" squares |
| B | | | *Cut for each fabric* |
| C | | | |
| D | | | |
| A | **Block 4** ¼ yard **each** of four fabrics | 3* | 8" squares |
| B | | | *Cut for each fabric* |
| C | | | |
| D | | | |
| **BORDERS** | | | |
| | Accent Border ⅓ yard | 5 | 2" x 42" |
| | Outside Border and Binding 1⅙ yards | 5 6 | 4½" x 42" 2¾" x 42" |
| Backing - 3 yards Batting - 54" x 66" | | | |

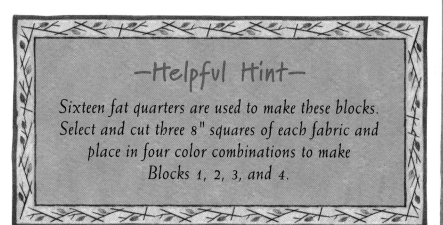

## —Helpful Hint—

*Sixteen fat quarters are used to make these blocks. Select and cut three 8" squares of each fabric and place in four color combinations to make Blocks 1, 2, 3, and 4.*

## Getting Started

Simple blocks made of quarter-square triangles form this colorful quilt. The top consists of forty-eight blocks measuring 6½" square unfinished. This simple block is made in four different color combinations. Each combination is repeated twelve times–half of which are a mirror image. It is important to sew an accurate seam allowance (page 92). Whenever possible, use the Assembly Line Method on page 92. Press all block seams open.

## Making the Blocks

**1.** Draw a diagonal line on wrong side of one 8" Block 1, Fabric A square. Place marked Fabric A square and one 8" Block 1, Fabric B square, right sides together. Sew scant ¼" away from drawn line on both sides to make half-square triangles. Make three matching units. Cut on drawn line and press seams open. This will make six half-square A/B triangles for Block 1 unit.

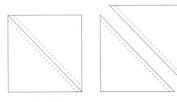

A = 8" × 8"
B = 8" × 8"
Make 3

Block I Unit

Make 6
Block I

**2.** Repeat step 1 to make six half-square triangles for each A/B combination for Block 2, Block 3, and Block 4 units.

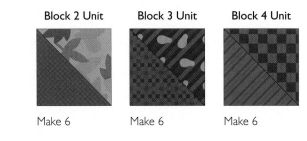

Block 2 Unit  Block 3 Unit  Block 4 Unit

Make 6      Make 6      Make 6

**3.** Draw a diagonal line on wrong side of one 8" Block 1, Fabric C square. Place marked Fabric C square and one 8" Block 1, Fabric D square right sides together. Sew scant ¼" away from drawn line on both sides to make half-square triangles. Make three matching units. Cut on drawn line and press seams open. This will make six half-square C/D triangles for Block 1 units.

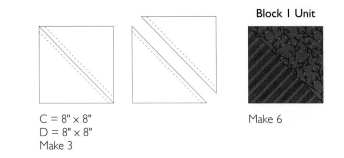

Block I Unit

C = 8" × 8"
D = 8" × 8"
Make 3

Make 6

**4.** Repeat step 3 to make six half-square triangles for each C/D combination for Block 2, Block 3, and Block 4 units.

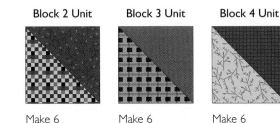

Block 2 Unit  Block 3 Unit  Block 4 Unit

Make 6      Make 6      Make 6

**5.** Draw a diagonal line on wrong side of one Block 1 unit from step 1 in opposite direction from seam as shown. Place marked unit, right sides together with one Block 1 unit from step 3 placing Fabric A triangle on top of Fabric C triangle. Sew scant ¼" away from drawn line on both sides. Make six using Block 1 units. Cut on drawn line and press seams open. Square to 6½". This will make twelve quarter-square triangles, six of each combination. Sort and label blocks, Block 1 and Block 1 R (reversed) as shown.

Unit from step 1
Unit from step 3
Make 6

**Block 1**

**Block 1R**

Make 12
(six of each variation)
Square to 6½"
Block 1 and 1R

**6.** Repeat step 5 to make quarter-square triangles using units from steps 2 and 4 for Block 2, Block 3, and Block 4. Sort and label each combination Block 2, 2R, 3, 3R, 4, or 4R as shown.

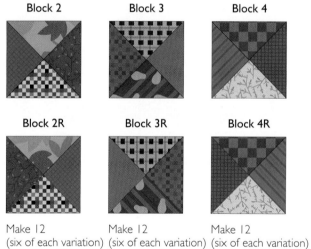

**Block 2**   **Block 3**   **Block 4**

**Block 2R**   **Block 3R**   **Block 4R**

Make 12          Make 12          Make 12
(six of each variation)  (six of each variation)  (six of each variation)
Square to 6½"    Square to 6½"    Square to 6½"
Block 2 and 2R   Block 3 and 3R   Block 4 and 4R

## Assembly

**1.** Referring to photo and layout on pages 64 and 65, arrange and sew blocks together to make eight horizontal rows of six blocks each. Press seams in opposite directions from row to row.

**2.** Referring to photo and layout on pages 64 and 65, sew rows together. Press seams in one direction.

## Adding the Borders

**1.** Sew 2" x 42" Accent Border strips together end-to-end to make one continuous 2"-wide Accent Border strip. Press. Refer to Adding the Borders on page 94. Measure quilt through center from side to side. Trim two 2"-wide Accent Border strips to that measurement. Sew to top and bottom of quilt. Press seams toward border.

**2.** Measure quilt through center from top to bottom including borders just added. Trim two 2"-wide Accent Border strips to this measurement. Sew to sides of quilt and press.

**3.** Repeat steps 1 and 2 to join, measure, trim, and sew 4½"-wide Outside Border strips to top, bottom, and sides of quilt. Press.

## Layering & Finishing

**1.** Cut backing in half crosswise. Sew pieces together to make one 54" x 80" (approximate) backing piece. Press and trim to 54" x 66".

**2.** Arrange and baste backing, batting, and top together referring to Layering the Quilt on page 94.

**3.** Machine or hand quilt.

**4.** Sew 2¾" binding strips end-to-end to make one continuous 2¾"-wide strip. Refer to Binding the Quilt on page 95 and bind quilt to finish.

# Autumn Leaves Centerpiece

The warmth and textures of an autumn afternoon are captured perfectly in this unique painted bowl. The deep rich color is achieved with sponging and glaze and dimensional leaves are easy to do with a stencil and a special paint.

## Materials Needed

Wooden Bowl

Multipurpose Spray Primer

Acrylic Craft Paints -

**Delta Ceramcoat®:** Spice Tan, Raw Sienna, Autumn Brown, Burnt Umber, Maple Sugar Tan, and Light Avocado

Assorted Paint Brushes

Sea Sponge

Delta Texture Magic™ Dimensional Paint

Plastic or Metal Palette Knife

Leaf Stencil (a simple plastic craft stencil works well) and Brush

Matte Spray Varnish

Antiquing Medium

Scotch® Magic™ Tape

Disposable Plate or Paper Palette

Sandpaper - Extra fine

## Painting the Bowl

*Note: allow bowl to dry thoroughly between each painting step.*

**1.** Lightly sand bowl and spray with primer. Allow to dry.

**2.** Paint inside of bowl with Autumn Brown paint and allow to dry.

**3.** Dampen sea sponge with water and wring thoroughly. Place small amounts of Autumn Brown and Maple Sugar Tan paints on a disposable plate or paper palette. Dip sea sponge in each color and blot paint by tapping on a paper towel several times. Using a tapping motion, sponge paint onto the inside of the bowl over the Autumn Brown basecoat. Use a light touch to achieve a stippled effect. Refill sponge as necessary, and adjust amount of each color on the sponge to achieve the desired effect. Allow to dry.

**4.** Paint outside of bowl with Spice Tan paint. When dry, refer to step 3 and sponge with Raw Sienna and Burnt Umber paint colors. Use a very light touch for a subtle texture.

**5.** Paint rim of bowl with Light Avocado paint and allow to dry.

**6.** Using Scotch® Magic™ Tape, tape leaf stencil to bowl. Using a palette knife and Texture Magic™ Dimensional Paint, spread paint over the stencil design, carefully holding stencil tightly against the bowl.

**7.** While dimensional paint is still wet, carefully lift stencil away from bowl so not to smudge paint.

**8.** Allow dimensional paint to dry before moving to next area to repeat the process. Wash and dry stencil between each application.

**9.** When dimensional leaves are dry, apply Avocado paint with dry brush technique. Use clean stencil to mask bowl by taping stencil over a dimensional leaf. Using a stiff brush such as a stencil brush, and a circular motion, apply paint. Use more pressure on outside edges of stencil so less paint is applied toward the middle of leaf shape. Allow to dry. Repeat dry brush process for each leaf shape.

**10.** When thoroughly dry, spray with matte varnish.

**11.** Apply antiquing medium to entire bowl, wiping medium off top edges of leaves so that they stand out from background.

**12.** When dry, apply one to two more coats of spray matte varnish. We filled the bowl with an unusual mix of faux fruit, balls of yarn, skeins of thread, and dried leaves.

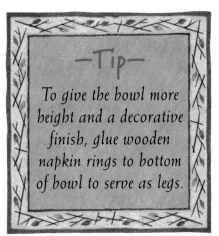

—Tip—

*To give the bowl more height and a decorative finish, glue wooden napkin rings to bottom of bowl to serve as legs.*

# Pumpkin Patch

*Plump pumpkins are perfect to decorate an Autumn porch and these gorgeous gourds will last for years with their faux finishes and wooden leaves. Craft store pumpkins receive painted finishes, real wood stems, and raffia-tied leaves for a decorative look.*

10¢ lb.

## Materials Needed

Two Foam Pumpkins
All Purpose Spray Primer
Acrylic Craft Paints -
 **Americana®**: Burnt Orange,
 Pumpkin, and Burnt Sienna
 **Delta Ceramcoat®**: Burnt
 Umber, Light Avocado, and
 Avocado
Burnt Umber Glaze
Four Unfinished Wooden Leaves
Sandpaper
Disposable Plate or Paper Palette
Sharp Knife
Old Toothbrush
Assorted Paintbrushes
Sea Sponge
Crackle Medium
Matte Spray Varnish
Raffia
Twigs

## Painting the Pumpkins

For interest, a sponged technique was used on one pumpkin and a crackle technique was used on the other.

**1.** Spray both pumpkins with primer and allow to dry.

**2.** For the sponged pumpkin, basecoat the pumpkin with Burnt Orange paint and allow to dry.

**3.** Dampen sea sponge with water and wring thoroughly. Place small amounts of Burnt Sienna and Burnt Orange paints on a disposable plate or paper palette. Dip sea sponge in both colors and blot paint by tapping on a paper towel several times. Using a tapping motion, sponge paint onto pumpkin to darken color. Use a light touch to achieve a stippled effect. Refill sponge as necessary, and adjust amount of each color on the sponge to achieve the desired effect. Allow to dry.

**4.** Highlight the pumpkin by using the same sponging technique and Burnt Orange and Pumpkin paint colors. Allow to dry.

**5.** For the crackled pumpkin, basecoat pumpkin with Burnt Umber paint and allow to dry.

**6.** Following manufacturer's directions, apply crackle medium to pumpkin and allow to "set" according to manufacturer's specifications.

**7.** Apply a quick, even coat of Burnt Orange paint to the pumpkin. Crackles will appear in the painted surface. Do not touch as surface is very fragile when wet. Allow to dry thoroughly.

**8.** Spray both pumpkins with matte varnish and allow to dry.

**9.** Following manufacturer's directions, apply Burnt Umber Glaze to both pumpkins allowing more glaze to gather in depressions.

**10.** Spray pumpkins with one or two additional coats of matte varnish.

**11.** Using a sharp knife, cut a hole in "stem" of each pumpkin. Insert a wood twig into the hole for a stem.

**12.** Drill a hole in the stem of each wooden leaf. If needed, sand leaves and remove residue with a damp cloth.

**13.** Paint two leaves with Avocado paint and two with Light Avocado paint. Allow to dry.

**14.** Spray with matte varnish.

**15.** Spatter leaves with Burnt Umber paint by mixing a small amount of paint with a few drops of water. Fill an old toothbrush with paint mixture, then run your thumb over the bristles. Practice this technique on a piece of paper before trying it on your leaves. If some spatters are too large, remove while wet with a cotton swab. Allow to dry then spray with matte varnish.

**16.** Apply Burnt Umber Glaze to leaves. When dry, apply a final coat of spray varnish.

**17.** Tie leaves to twig stem of pumpkin with raffia.

# Winter

Winter's warmth
is found within—
within the home,
the hearth,
the heart

Warm up winter with beautiful quilts
and comfy pillows perfect for relaxing
and enjoying a crackling fire and
good book. Piping hot tea on a painted
tray makes winter go away.

# Winter Star Lap Quilt

*Finished Size: 59½" x 59½*

Subtle stars form a constellation of ethereal color in this cozy quilt that's the essence of winter's quiet landscape. Sparks of color are hushed with a blanket of neutrals for the perfect quilt to match all décors. Speed piecing methods including Speedy Triangles and Quarter-Square Triangles make this quilt a fast and fun project for a cold winter's day.

# Fabric Requirements and Cutting Instructions

Read all instructions before beginning and use ¼"-wide seam allowances throughout. Read Cutting Strips and Pieces on page 92 prior to cutting fabrics.

| Winter Star Lap Quilt 59½" x 59½" | FIRST CUT | | SECOND CUT | |
|---|---|---|---|---|
| | Number of Strips or Pieces | Dimensions | Number of Pieces | Dimensions |
| **Fabric A** Background 1⅔ yards | 3 | 6" x 42" | 16 | 6" squares |
| | 5 | 5½" x 42" | 32 | 5½" squares |
| | 4 | 2½" x 42" | 64 | 2½" squares |
| **Fabric B** Block 1 Triangles and Block 2 Squares ¼ yard each for eight fabrics | 1* | 6" square* | Block 1 | |
| | 2* | 5½" squares* | Block 1 | |
| | 1* | 4½" square* | Block 2 | |
| | 4* | 2½" squares* | Block 2 | |
| | | *Cut for each fabric* | | |
| **Fabric C** Block 2 Triangles and Block 1 Squares ¼ yard each for eight fabrics | 1* | 6" square* | Block 2 | |
| | 2* | 5½" squares* | Block 2 | |
| | 1* | 4½" square* | Block 1 | |
| | 4* | 2½" squares* | Block 1 | |
| | | *Cut for each fabric* | | |
| **BORDERS** | | | | |
| **First Border** ⅓ yard | 5 | 1¾" x 42" | | |
| **Second Border** ⅜ yard | 6 | 1½" x 42" "fussy cut" | | |
| **Outside Border** ⅔ yard | 6 | 3½" x 42" | | |
| **Binding** ⅝ yard | 7 | 2¾" x 42" | | |

Backing - 3⅝ yards
Batting - 64" x 64"

## Winter Star Lap Quilt

*Finished Size: 59½" x 59½"*

## Getting Started

This scrappy quilt has a unique pattern to it. It consists of sixteen pieced blocks measuring 12½" square unfinished. Even though stripes and plaids are used, simple piecing techniques make block assembly easy. Block 1 and Block 2 are made from the same fabric combinations, but the placement of the squares and triangles is reversed as well as the pressing direction. For our quilt, we placed all directional fabric stripes in the same direction. **It is recommend that you make one each of these two blocks first before proceeding with all sixteen blocks.** Then place remaining block pieces in fourteen stacks according to the block layout and use an assembly line method to piece the blocks.

Refer to Accurate Seam Allowance on page 92. Whenever possible, use the Assembly Line Method page 92. Press seams in direction of arrows.

# Making the Blocks

**1.** Make Speedy Triangles by drawing two intersecting diagonal lines on wrong side of one 6" Fabric A square with a pencil as shown. Draw perpendicular lines in center of square. Place marked Fabric A square right sides together with one 6" Fabric B square. Sew a scant ¼" away from diagonal lines on both sides of lines. Cut on all drawn lines. Press seams toward Fabric B. Square units to 2½". This makes eight half-square triangles. Make eight identical units for each Block 1.

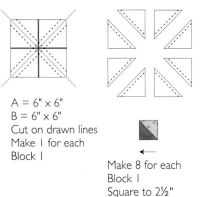

A = 6" × 6"
B = 6" × 6"
Cut on drawn lines
Make 1 for each
Block 1

←
Make 8 for each
Block 1
Square to 2½"

**2.** Repeat step 1 using 6" Fabric A and Fabric C squares pressing seams toward Fabric A. Make eight identical units for each Block 2.

A = 6" × 6"
C = 6" × 6"
Cut on drawn lines
Make 1 for each Block 2

→
Make 8 for each
Block 2
Square to 2½"

**3.** Sew one unit from step 1 to one 2½" Fabric A square as shown, Press. Make four for each Block 1.

2½

←
Make 4 for each Block 1

Sew one unit from step 1 to one 2½" Fabric C square as shown. When Fabric C is directional, sew two Fabric C squares vertically and two horizontally. Press. Make four for each Block 1.

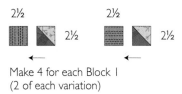

2½          2½
2½          2½

←                    ←
Make 4 for each Block 1
(2 of each variation)

**4.** Sew one unit from step 2 to one 2½" Fabric A square as shown, Press. Make four for each Block 2.

2½

→
Make 4 for each Block 2

Sew one unit from step 2 to one 2½" Fabric B square as shown. When Fabric B is directional, sew two Fabric B squares vertically and two squares horizontally. Press. Make four for each Block 2.

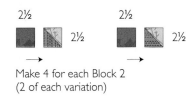

2½          2½
2½          2½

→          →
Make 4 for each Block 2
(2 of each variation)

**5.** Sew units from step 3, one of each combination, together in pairs as shown. Press. Make four for each Block 1.

**Block 1 Unit**

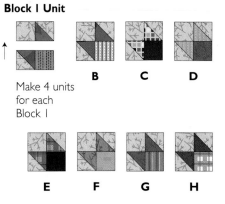

Make 4 units
for each
Block 1

B          C          D

E          F          G          H

**6.** Sew units from step 4, one of each combination, together in pairs as shown. Press. Make four for each Block 2.

**Block 2 Unit**

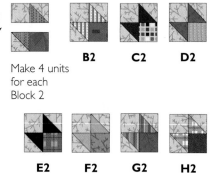

Make 4 units
for each
Block 2

B2          C2          D2

E2          F2          G2          H2

**7.** Make half-square triangles by drawing a diagonal line on wrong side of one 5½" Fabric A square. Place marked square right sides together with one 5½" Fabric B square. Sew a scant ¼" away from drawn line on both sides as shown. Cut on drawn line. Press. This will make two half-square triangles.

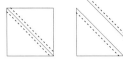 

A = 5½" × 5½"
B = 5½" × 5½"
Make 2 for each block

→
Make 4 for
each Block 1

**8.** Make quarter-square triangle units by drawing a diagonal line on wrong side of one unit from step 7 in opposite direction from seam as shown. Place marked unit right sides together with matching unit from step 7, placing Fabric A triangle on top of Fabric B triangle. Sew a scant ¼" away from drawn line on both sides. Cut on drawn line as shown. Press seams toward Fabric B, twisting center intersection. Square unit to 4½". This will make two quarter-square triangle units. Repeat steps 7 and 8 to make four quarter-square triangle units for each Block 1.

**Block I Unit**

Units from step 5
Make 2 for each Block I

**A**

Make 4 units for each Block I
Square to 4½

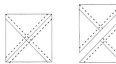

B     C     D     E     F     G     H

**9.** Repeat steps 7 and 8 to make quarter-square triangle units using 5½" Fabric A and C squares as shown. Press seams toward Fabric A. Make four units for Block 2. Repeat to make four quarter-square triangles for each Block 2.

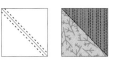

**Block 2 Unit**

A = 5½" × 5½"
C = 5½" × 5½"
Make 2 for each block

Make 4 for
each Block 2

**A2**

Make 4 units for each Block 2
Square to 4

B2     C2     D2     E2     F2     G2     H2

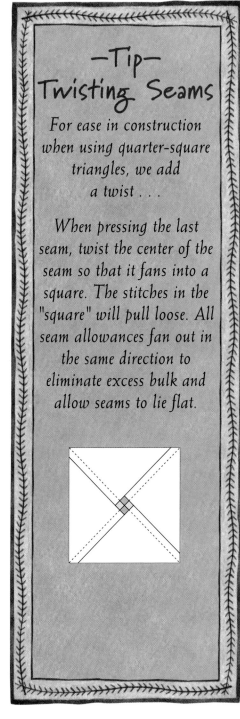

*—Tip—*
*Twisting Seams*

*For ease in construction when using quarter-square triangles, we add a twist . . .*

*When pressing the last seam, twist the center of the seam so that it fans into a square. The stitches in the "square" will pull loose. All seam allowances fan out in the same direction to eliminate excess bulk and allow seams to lie flat.*

**10.** Sew one unit from step 8 between two matching units from step 5 as shown. Press. Make two units for each Block 1. Sew one unit from step 9 between two matching units from step 6 as shown. Press. Make two units for each Block 2.

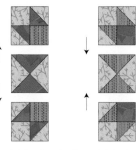

Make 2 units for     Make 2 units for
each Block 1          each Block 2

**11.** Sew one 4½" Fabric C square between two matching units from step 8 as shown. Press. Make one unit for each Block 1. Sew one 4½" Fabric B square between two matching units from step 9 as shown. Press. Make one unit for each Block 2.

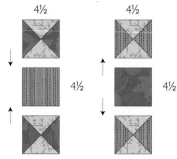

Make 1 unit for     Make 1 unit for
each Block 1          each Block 2

**12.** Sew one unit from step 11 between two matching units from step 10 as shown. Press. Block measures 12½" square. Repeat to make Block 2 using Block 2 units.

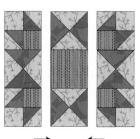
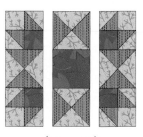

Block 1 measures 12½" square        Block 2 measures 12½" square

**13.** Make eight of each Block 1. Blocks measure 12½" square.

**Block 1**

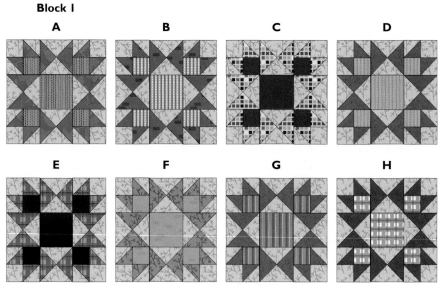

A          B          C          D

E          F          G          H

Blocks measure 12  " square

**14.** Make eight of each Block 2. Blocks measure 12½" square.

**Block 2**

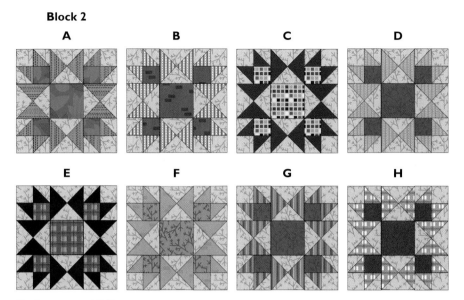

Blocks measure 12½" square

## Assembly

**1.** Referring to photo and layout on pages 74 and 75, arrange blocks in four horizontal rows of four blocks each. Press seams in opposite directions from row to row.

**2.** Sew rows together and press.

## Adding the Borders

**1.** Sew 1¾" x 42" First Border strips end-to-end to make one continuous 1¾"-wide strip. Press. Refer to Adding the Borders on page 94. Measure quilt through center from side to side. Cut two 1¾"-wide First Border strips to that measurement. Sew to top and bottom of quilt. Press seams toward border.

**2.** Measure quilt through center from top to bottom including borders just added. Cut two 1¾"-wide First Border strips to that measurement. Sew to sides of quilt. Press.

**3.** Refer to steps 1 and 2 to join, measure, trim, and sew 1½"-wide Second Border and 3½"-wide Outside Border strips to top, bottom, and sides of quilt. Press seams toward each newly added border strip.

## Layering and Finishing

**1.** Cut backing crosswise into two equal pieces. Sew pieces together to make one (approximate) 65" x 80" backing piece. Trim backing to 65" x 65" and press.

**2.** Arrange and baste backing, batting, and top together referring to Layering the Quilt on page 94.

**3.** Hand or machine quilt as desired.

**4.** Sew 2¾" binding strips end-to-end to make one continuous 2¾"-wide strip. Refer to Binding the Quilt on page 95 and bind quilt to finish.

# Fabric Requirements and Cutting Instructions

Read all instructions before beginning and use ¼"-wide seam allowances throughout. Read Cutting Strips and Pieces on page 92 prior to cutting fabrics.

| Winter Star Bed Quilt 80" x 104" | FIRST CUT | | SECOND CUT | |
|---|---|---|---|---|
| | Number of Strips or Pieces | Dimensions | Number of Pieces | Dimensions |
| **Fabric A** Background 3⅝ yards | 6 | 6" x 42" | 36 | 6" squares |
| | 11 | 5½" x 42" | 72 | 5½" squares |
| | 9 | 2½" x 42" | 144 | 2½" squares |
| **Fabric B** Block 1 Triangles and Block 2 Squares ⅜ yard each for nine fabrics | 2* | 6" squares* | | Block 1 |
| | 4* | 5½" squares* | | Block 1 |
| | 2* | 4½" squares* | | Block 2 |
| | 8* | 2½" squares* | | Block 2 |
| | | *Cut for each fabric* | | |
| **Fabric C** Block 2 Triangles and Block 1 Squares ⅜ yard each for nine fabrics | 2* | 6" squares* | | Block 2 |
| | 4* | 5½" squares* | | Block 2 |
| | 2* | 4½" squares* | | Block 1 |
| | 8* | 2½" squares* | | Block 1 |
| | | *Cut for each fabric* | | |
| **BORDERS** | | | | |
| **First Border** ⅝ yard | 8 | 2½" x 42" | | |
| **Second Border and Binding** 1⅛ yards | 10 | 2¾" x 42" *(binding)* | | |
| | 8 | 1" x 42" | | |
| **Third Border** ½ yard | 8 | 1½" x 42" "fussy cut" | | |
| **Outside Border** 1¾ yards | 9 | 6½" x 42" | | |

Backing - 7⅓ yards
Batting - 88" x 112"

# Getting Started

We've doubled the blocks and added two more fabrics to expand the Winter Star Lap Quilt into a queen-size bed quilt. The quilt consists of thirty-five blocks measuring 12½" unfinished. Cutting instructions are for thirty-six blocks. It is recommended to make all thirty-six blocks and use the extra for an accent pillow or other project. Refer to Accurate Seam Allowance on page 92. Whenever possible, use the Assembly Line Method on page 92. Press seams in direction of arrows.

## Winter Star Bed Quilt

## Making the Blocks

**1.** Refer to Winter Star Lap Quilt, pages 75–78, steps 1-12, for instructions to make eighteen of Block 1, two for each fabric. Make eighteen of Block 2, two for each fabric. Refer to pages 78 and 79, steps 13 and 14, for individual block layouts. New fabric combination is shown below.

**Block 1**

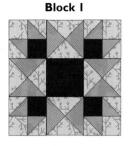

**Block 2**

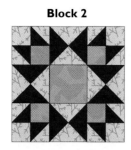

Blocks measure 12½" square

**2.** Referring to layout, arrange and sew blocks in seven horizontal rows of five blocks each. Press seams in opposite directions from row to row.

**3.** Sew rows together. Press.

## Adding the Borders

**1.** Sew 2½" x 42" First Border strips together end-to-end to make one continuous 2½"-wide border strip. Press. Measure quilt through center from side to side. Cut two 2½"-wide border strips to this measurement. Sew to top and bottom of quilt. Press seams toward border.

**2.** Measure quilt through center from top to bottom including borders just added. Cut two 2½"-wide First Border strips to this measurement. Sew to sides of quilt. Press.

**3.** Refer to steps 1 and 2 to join, measure, trim, and sew 1"-wide Second Border, 1½"-wide Third Border and 6½"-wide Outside Border strips to top, bottom, and sides of quilt. Press.

## Winter Star Bed Quilt

*Finished Size: 80" x 104"*

## Layering and Finishing

**1.** Cut backing crosswise in three equal pieces. Sew pieces together to make one 88" x 120" (approximate) backing piece. Press.

**2.** Arrange and baste backing, batting, and top together referring to Layering the Quilt on page 94.

**3.** Machine or hand quilt as desired.

**4.** Sew 2¾"-wide binding strips end-to-end to make one continuous 2¾"-wide binding strip. Refer to Binding the Quilt on page 95 and bind quilt to finish.

# Winter Comfort Pillow

Finished Size: 18″ x 1

An "X" marks the spot for cozy winter comfort.
This attractive pillow is subtle enough for many uses
and intricate enough to provide decorating panache.
Make several for a day bed or couch or warm up
a window seat with stylish comfort.

# Fabric Requirements and Cutting Instructions

Read all instructions before beginning and use ¼"-wide seam allowances throughout. Read Cutting Strips and Pieces on page 92 prior to cutting fabrics.

| Winter Comfort Pillow 18" x 18" | FIRST CUT | | SECOND CUT | |
|---|---|---|---|---|
| | Number of Strips or Pieces | Dimensions | Number of Pieces | Dimensions |
| **Fabric A** Background ¼ yard | 3 | 2½" x 42" | 2 | 2½" x 10½" |
| | | | 4 | 2½" x 6½" |
| | | | 4 | 2½" x 4½" |
| | | | 6 | 2½" squares |
| **Fabric B** Light Accent ⅙ yard | 1 | 3½" x 42" | 7 | 3½" squares |
| **Fabric C** Dark Accent ⅙ yard | 1 | 3½" x 42" | 7 | 3½" squares |
| **First Border & Backing** ½ yard | 1 | 12" x 42" | 2 | 12" x 18½" (backing) |
| | 2 | 2" x 42" | 2 | 2" x 17½" |
| | | | 2 | 2" x 14½" |
| **Outside Border** ⅛ yard | 2 | 1" x 42" | 2 | 1" x 18½" |
| | | | 2 | 1" x 17½" |
| Batting and Lining - ⅔ yard (22½" square of each) 18" Pillow Form | | | | |

# Getting Started

Quarter-square triangles and background fabric form an easily pieced 14½" (unfinished) quilt block. Coordinating borders and backing complete the pillow. If using a striped fabric for Fabric B, note placement of stripe orientation in steps 3 through 7.

# Making the Pillow Top

**1.** Make half-square triangles by drawing a diagonal line on wrong side of one 3½" Fabric B square. Place marked square right sides together with one 3½" Fabric C square. Sew a scant ¼" away from drawn line on both sides as shown. Cut on drawn line. Press. Make seven. This will make fourteen half square triangles.

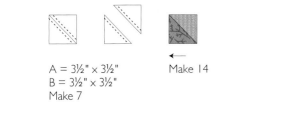

A = 3½" x 3½"
B = 3½" x 3½"
Make 7

Make 14

## Winter Comfort Pillow

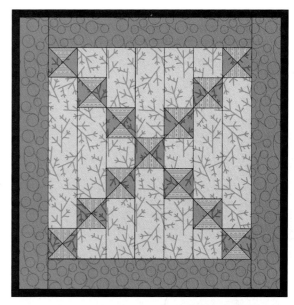

*Finished Size: 18" x 18"*

**2.** Make quarter-square triangle units by drawing a diagonal line on wrong side of one unit from step 1 in opposite direction from seam as shown. Place marked unit right sides together with another unit from step 1, placing Fabric B triangle on top of Fabric C triangle. Sew a scant ¼" away from drawn line on both sides as shown. Make seven. Cut on drawn line. Press seams toward Fabric C, twisting center intersection. See tip box on page 77. Square to 2½". Make fourteen. You will use only thirteen quarter-square triangle units. If a striped fabric is used, stripes will be in two directions.

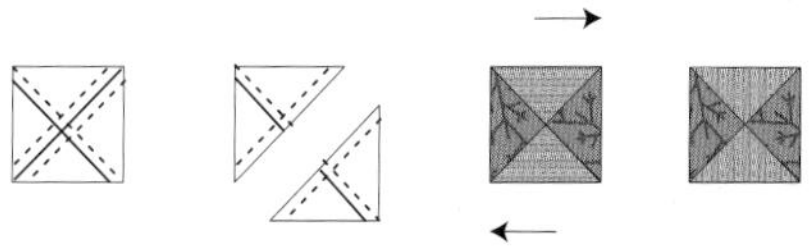

Unit from Step 1 Make 7

Square to 2½" Make 14

**3.** Sew one 2½" x 10½" Fabric A piece between two units from step 2 noting direction of stripes, as shown. Press. Make two.

10½

2½

Make 2

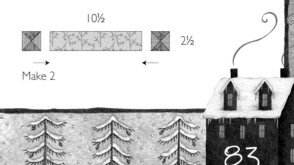

**4.** Sew together two 2½" Fabric A squares, two units from step 2, and one 2½" x 6½" Fabric A piece as shown. Press. Make two.

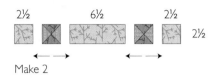

Make 2

**5.** Sew together two 2½" x 4½" Fabric A pieces, two units from step 2, and one 2½" Fabric A square as shown. Press. Make two.

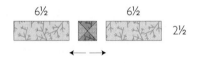

Make 2

**6.** Sew one unit from step 2 between two 2½" x 6½" Fabric A pieces as shown. Press.

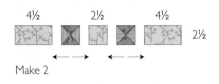

**7.** Sew together units from steps 3, 4, 5, and 6 as shown, noting direction of stripes. Press. Block measures 14½" square.

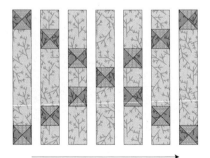

Block measures 14½" square

**8.** Sew block from step 7 between two 2" x 14½" Fabric D pieces as shown. Press. Sew 2" x 17½" Fabric D pieces to sides. Press.

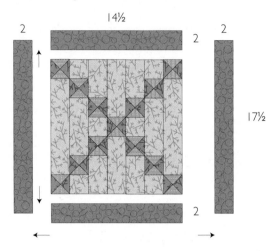

**9.** Sew unit from step 8 between two 1" x 17½" Outside Border strips. Press. Sew 1" x 18½" Outside Border strips to sides. Press.

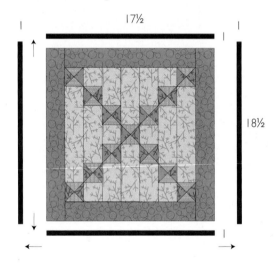

## Layering and Finishing

Refer to Finishing Pillows, page 95, step 1, to quilt pillow top. Refer to steps 2-4 to sew 12" x 18½" Fabric D backing pieces to pillow. Insert 18" pillow form.

# —Decorating with Pillows—

Create a warm and welcoming winter haven by piling on the pillows! This day bed is decked with soft, comfortable pillows in a variety of fabrics and styles. Fleece and wool are natural choices to create a feeling of toasty warmth and the look of luxurious textures. Teamed with a chenille embroidered silk pillow, this assortment of pillows provides cuddly comfort on a cold winter day.

Striped fleece fabric is perfect for over-sized pillows. Simply cut fabric for front side of pillow 1" larger than pillow form on all sides. Refer to Finishing Pillows on page 95 to cut and sew pillow back. Use ½" seams when sewing fleece. For the red pillow, simply sew together two 10½" wool squares, turn, stuff, and hand-stitch opening closed.

Solid color green wool pillows and the embroidered pillow were purchased at various department stores.

A combination of fleece and cotton was used for the button pillow. Quilt solid tan fleece using a zigzag stitch and brown thread. Add mitered borders using a cotton fabric for a decorative touch. A variety of brown buttons add fun detail to this primitive pillow.

Pillows are quick to stitch and can be as simple or elaborate as desired. Have fun experimenting with various techniques and mixing styles and fabrics for cozy combinations.

# Cozy Pines Quilt

**Quick!**

Finished Size: 50" x 61

Wool trees and stars dot a snowy flannel field making this quaint quilt a snow season necessity. Simple and easy to make, this quilt is warm and cozy, cute and cuddly! It would make a great gift for anyone on your list.

# Fabric Requirements and Cutting Instructions

Read all instructions before beginning and use ¼"-wide seam allowances throughout. Read Cutting Strips and Pieces on page 92 prior to cutting fabrics.

| Cozy Pines Quilt 50" x 61" | FIRST CUT | | SECOND CUT | |
|---|---|---|---|---|
| | Number of Strips or Pieces | Dimensions | Number of Pieces | Dimensions |
| **Center Panel** 1⅓ yards | 1 | 33½" x 44½" | | |
| **BORDERS** | | | | |
| **First Border** ⅓ yard | 5 | 1½" x 42" | | |
| **Second Border** ⅝ yard | 5 | 3½" x 42" | | |
| **Outside Border** 1⅞ yards | 2 / 2 | 65" x 4½"* / 54" x 4½"* *(fussy cut)* | | |
| **Binding** ⅝ yard | 6 | 2¾" x 42" | | |

**Backing** - 3⅛ yards
**Batting** - 56" x 67"
**Tree Appliqués** - ½ yard wool or WoolFelt®
**Star Appliqués** - ⅓ yard wool or WoolFelt®
**Lightweight Fusible Web** - 1 yard

*For directional fabric, the size that is listed first runs parallel to selvage.*

## Cozy Pines Quilt

*Finished Size: 50" x 61"*

# Getting Started

This cozy flannel quilt is fast, easy to make, and a must to keep you warm this winter. The large center panel has appliquéd wool trees and stars scattered about and is surrounded by multiple borders. "Fussy Cut" the Outside Border to match stripes. Refer to page 61 for directions on felting wool.

# Assembly

**1.** Refer to Adding the Borders on page 94. Measure quilt through center from side to side. Cut two 1½" x 42" First Border strips to that measurement. Sew to top and bottom of quilt. Press seams toward border.

**2.** Sew remaining 1½" x 42" First Border strips end-to-end to make one continuous 1½"-wide strip. Press. Measure quilt through center from top to bottom, including borders just added. Cut two 1½"-wide First Border strips to that measurement and sew to sides of quilt. Press.

**3.** Refer to steps 1 and 2 to join, measure, trim, and sew 3½"-wide Second Border strips to top, bottom, and sides of quilt. Press seams toward Second Border.

**4.** Refer to Mitered Borders on page 94. Sew 54" x 4½" Outside Border strips to top and bottom and 65" x 4½" Outside Border strips to sides of quilt, mitering corners. Press seams toward Outside Border.

## Adding the Appliqués

Refer to appliqué instructions on page 93. Our instructions are for Quick Fuse Appliqué, but if you prefer to use cotton fabric and hand appliqué, add ¼"-wide seam allowances. Felt and Woolfelt® can be hand appliquéd without turning edges.

**1.** Referring to Quick-Fuse Appliqué on page 93, trace Tree and Star patterns onto paper side of fusible web. Use Tree and Star Appliqué fabrics to prepare eight trees and eleven stars for fusing.

**2.** Refer to photo and layout on pages 86 and 87. Position and fuse appliqués on quilt. Refer to Embroidery Stitch Guide on page 95 and use a blanket stitch to machine or hand-stitch trees to quilt.

**3.** Using a straight stitch, machine or hand-stitch stars to quilt, stitching through center from point to point as shown.

## Layering and Finishing

**1.** Cut backing crosswise into two equal pieces. Sew pieces together to make one 56" x 80" (approximate) backing piece. Press and trim to 56" x 67".

**2.** Arrange and baste backing, batting, and top together referring to Layering the Quilt on page 94. Hand or machine quilt as desired.

**3.** Sew 2¾"-wide binding strips end-to-end to make one continuous 2¾"-wide strip. Refer to Binding the Quilt on page 95 and bind quilt to finish.

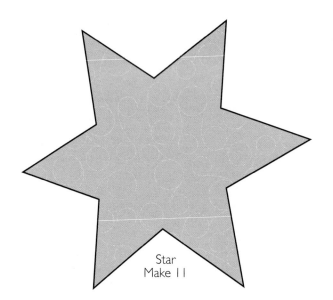

Star
Make 11

**Cozy Pines
Appliqué Patterns**

Tracing Line ———————

Pine Tree
Make 8

# Tray For All Seasons

This useful and attractive tray will come in handy during any season of the year. A combination of paint, caulk, and decoupage gives the tray an interesting mix of dimension and texture and provides the opportunity to experiment with several techniques. Glazing blends the colors and techniques for a beautiful finish.

## Materials Needed

Purchased Wooden Tray*

Acrylic Craft Paints -

**Americana®:** Buttermilk, Antique White, Hauser Dark Green, Golden Straw

**Delta Ceramcoat®:** Medium Foliage Green, Raw Sienna, Cardinal Red, Barn Red, Spice Tan, Burnt Umber

Pencil and Ruler

Disposable Plate or Palette Paper

Sandpaper

Assorted Paintbrushes and Old Toothbrush

Decoupage Medium

Burnt Umber Glaze

Matte Spray Varnish

Decorator Products™ Decorator Tools™ Grout Tape

Green Fabric Scraps

Small Tube of Silicone Acrylic Caulking

Sea Sponge

*Unfinished trays are available at many craft stores or look for a previously painted tray at a thrift shop or import store.*

## Painting the Tray

*Note: Allow paint to dry thoroughly between all applications.*

**1.** Remove metal hardware (if any) from tray.

**2.** If tray is unfinished, sand well. If tray was previously painted, sand tray to remove all gloss and remove residue with tack cloth or damp cloth.

**3.** Referring to photo, use a pencil to draw vine line on inside or outside of tray wherever vine will be more visible. Knead caulking tube, then apply caulking along drawn line. It is okay to have thicker and thinner parts to the caulking line as this will add to the overall look. If you make a big mistake, wipe it off with a damp rag and try again. Caulking is used because it is flexible, adheres to most surfaces, and rarely cracks. Allow caulking to dry thoroughly.

**4.** Apply a basecoat of Buttermilk color paint to inside bottom of tray. Two coats may be necessary for good coverage.

**5.** Dampen sea sponge with water and wring thoroughly. Place small amounts of Buttermilk and Antique White paints on a disposable plate or paper palette. Dip sea sponge in each color and blot paint by tapping on a paper towel several times. Using a tapping motion, sponge paint onto the inside tray bottom. Use a light touch to achieve a stippled effect. Refill sponge as necessary, and adjust amount of each color on the sponge to achieve desired effect. Allow to dry.

**6.** Apply Medium Foliage Green paint to inside and outside sides of tray, painting over the caulking line.

**7.** Referring to photo, use ruler and pencil to divide bottom of tray into even squares or rectangles. Apply ¼" grout tape along these lines.

**8.** Use Cardinal Red, Golden Straw, Spice Tan, and Medium Foliage Green paints to paint rectangles or squares as desired. Allow to dry. Using the sponging method described in step 5, sponge a slightly darker paint color for each colored square concentrating on the edges. Use the following paint combinations: Cardinal Red/Barn Red, Golden Straw/Raw Sienna, Spice Tan/Burnt Umber, Medium Foliage Green/Hauser Dark Green.

**9.** When paint is thoroughly dry, remove grout tape to expose tan "grout" lines. Erase any unwanted pencil lines.

**10.** Paint top edge Barn Red. When thoroughly dry, lightly sand sides and top edge to distress.

**11.** Spray bottom and inside sides with matte varnish.

**12.** Using leaf pattern on page 15, cut leaves from green fabric and use decoupage medium to attach them to tray along vine line. When leaves are dry, apply several coats of decoupage medium to sides of tray, following directions on decoupage product. Allow to dry thoroughly.

**13.** Following manufacturer's directions, apply Burnt Umber Glaze to tray, allowing more glaze to gather around vine lines to give a shadowed effect. Add or remove glaze until the desired effect is achieved.

**14.** When tray is dry, apply several coats of matte varnish.

**15.** Reattach handles to tray.

# General Directions

## Cutting Strips & Pieces

We recommend washing cotton fabrics in cold water and pressing before making projects in this book. Using a rotary cutter, see-through ruler, and a cutting mat, cut the strips and pieces for the project. If indicated on the Cutting Chart, some will need to be cut again into smaller strips and pieces. Make second cuts in order shown to maximize use of fabric. The approximate width of the fabric is 42". Measurements for all pieces include ¼"-wide seam allowance unless otherwise indicated. Press in the direction of the arrows.

## Fussy Cut

To make a "fussy cut," carefully position ruler or template over a selected design in fabric. Include seam allowances before cutting desired pieces.

## Assembly Line Method

Whenever possible, use an assembly line method. Position pieces right sides together and line up next to sewing machine. Stitch first unit together, then continue sewing others without breaking threads. When all units are sewn, clip threads to separate. Press in direction of arrows.

## Accurate Seam Allowance

Accurate seam allowances are always important, but especially when the blocks contain many pieces and the quilt top contains multiple pieced borders. If each seam is off as little as ¹⁄₁₆", you'll soon find yourself struggling with components that just won't fit.

To ensure seams are a perfect ¼"-wide, try this simple test: Cut three strips of fabric, each exactly 1½" x 12". With right sides together, and long raw edges aligned, sew two strips together, carefully maintaining a ¼" seam. Press seam to one side. Add the third strip to complete the strip set. Press and measure. The finished strip set should measure 3½" x 12". The center strip should measure 1"-wide, the two outside strips 1¼"-wide, and the seam allowances exactly ¼".

If your measurements differ, check to make sure that seams have been pressed flat. If strip set still doesn't "measure up," try stitching a new strip set, adjusting the seam allowance until a perfect ¼"-wide seam is achieved.

Pressing is very important for accurate seam allowances. Press seams using either steam or dry heat with an "up and down" motion. Do not use side-to-side motion as this will distort the unit or block. Set the seam by pressing along the line of stitching, then press seams to one side as indicated by project instructions.

## Quick Corner Triangles

Quick corner triangles are formed by simply sewing fabric squares to other squares or rectangles. The directions and diagrams with each project illustrate what size pieces to use and where to place squares on the corresponding piece. Follow steps 1–3 below to make quick corner triangle units.

**1.** With pencil and ruler, draw diagonal line on wrong side of fabric square that will form the triangle. See Diagram A. This will be your sewing line.

A.

sewing line

**2.** With right sides together, place square on corresponding piece. Matching raw edges, pin in place, and sew ON drawn line. Trim off excess fabric, leaving ¼"-wide seam allowance as shown in Diagram B.

B.

trim ¼" away
from sewing line

**3.** Press seam in direction of arrow as shown in step-by-step project diagram. Measure completed quick corner triangle unit to ensure the greatest accuracy.

C.

finished
quick corner
triangle unit

# Quick-Fuse Appliqué

Quick-fuse appliqué is a method of adhering appliqué pieces to a background with fusible web. For quick and easy results, simply quick-fuse appliqué pieces in place. Use sewable, lightweight fusible web for the projects in this book unless otherwise indicated. Finishing raw edges with stitching is desirable; laundering is not recommended unless edges are finished.

**1.** With paper side up, lay fusible web over appliqué pattern. Leaving ½" space between pieces, trace all elements of design. Cut around traced pieces, approximately ¼" outside traced line. See Diagram A.

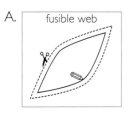

A. fusible web

**2.** With paper side up, position and press fusible web to wrong side of selected fabrics. Follow manufacturer's directions for iron temperature and fusing time. Cut out each piece on traced line. See Diagram B.

B. fabric-wrong side

**3.** Remove paper backing from pieces. A thin film will remain on wrong side of fabric. Position and fuse all pieces of one appliqué design at a time onto background, referring to photos for placement. Fused design will be the reverse of traced pattern.

# Appliqué Pressing Sheet

An appliqué pressing sheet is very helpful when there are many small elements to apply using a quick-fuse appliqué technique. The pressing sheet allows small items to be bonded together before applying them to the background. The sheet is coated with a special material that prevents fusible web from adhering permanently to the sheet. Follow manufacturer's directions. Remember to let fabric cool completely before lifting it from the appliqué sheet. If not cooled, the fusible web could remain on the sheet instead of on the fabric.

# Machine Appliqué

This technique should be used when you are planning to launder quick-fuse projects. Several different stitches can be used: small narrow zigzag stitch, satin stitch, blanket stitch, or another decorative machine stitch. Use an open toe appliqué foot if your machine has one. Use a stabilizer to obtain even stitches and help prevent puckering. Always practice first to check machine settings.

**1.** Fuse all pieces following Quick-Fuse Appliqué directions.

**2.** Cut a piece of stabilizer large enough to extend beyond the area to be stitched. Pin to the wrong side of fabric.

**3.** Select thread to match appliqué.

**4.** Following the order that appliqués were positioned, stitch along the edges of each section. Anchor beginning and ending stitches by tying off or stitching in place two or three times.

**5.** Complete all stitching, then remove stabilizer.

# Hand Appliqué

Hand appliqué is easy when you start out with the right supplies. Cotton and machine embroidery thread are easy to work with. Pick a color that matches the appliqué fabric as closely as possible. Use appliqué or silk pins for holding shapes in place and a long, thin needle, such as a sharp, for stitching.

**1.** Make a template for every shape in the appliqué design. Use a dotted line to show where pieces overlap.

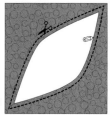

**2.** Place template on right side of appliqué fabric. Trace around template.

**3.** Cut out shapes ¼" beyond traced line.

**4.** Position shapes on background fabric, referring to quilt layout. Pin shapes in place.

**5.** When layering and stitching appliqué shapes, always work from background to foreground. Where shapes overlap, do not turn under and stitch edges of bottom pieces. Turn and stitch the edges of the piece on top.

**6.** Use the traced line as your turn-under guide. Entering from the wrong side of the appliqué shape, bring the needle up on the traced line. Using the tip of the needle, turn under the fabric along the traced line. Using blind stitch, stitch along the folded edge to join the appliqué shape to the back-ground fabric. Turn under and stitch about ¼" at a time.

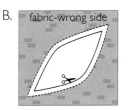

## Making Bias Strips

**1.** Refer to Fabric Requirements and Cutting Instructions for the amount of fabric required for the specific bias needed.

**2.** Remove selvages from the fabric piece and cut into a square. Mark edge with straight pin where selvages were removed as shown. Cut square once diagonally into two equal 45° triangles. (For larger squares, fold square in half diagonally and gently press fold. Open fabric square and cut on fold.)

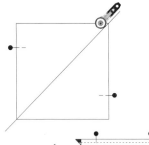

**3.** Place pinned edges right sides together and stitch along edge with a ¼" seam. Press seam open.

**4.** Using a ruler and rotary cutter, cut bias strips to width specified in quilt directions.

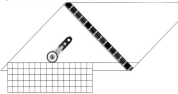

**5.** Each strip has a diagonal end. To join, place strips perpendicular to each other, right sides together, matching diagonal cut edges and allowing tips of angles to extend approximately ¼" beyond edges. Sew ¼"-wide seams. Continue stitching ends together to make the desired length. Press seams open. Cut strips into recommended lengths according to quilt directions.

## Adding the Borders

**1.** Measure quilt through the center from side to side. Trim two border strips to this measurement. Sew to top and bottom of quilt. Press seams toward border.

**2.** Measure quilt through the center from top to bottom, including borders added in step 1. Trim border strips to this measurement. Sew to sides and press. Repeat to add additional borders.

## Mitered Borders

A mitered border is usually "fussy cut" to highlight a motif or design. Borders are cut slightly longer than needed to allow for centering of a motif or matching corners.

**1.** Cut the border strips or strip sets as indicated for quilt.

**2.** Measure each side of the quilt and mark center with a pin. Fold each border strip in half crosswise to find its midpoint and mark with a pin. Using the side measurements, measure out from the midpoint and place a pin to show where the edges of the quilt will be.

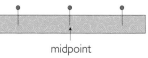

midpoint

**3.** Align a border strip to quilt. Pin at midpoints and pin-marked ends first, then along entire side, easing to fit if necessary.

**4.** Sew border to quilt, stopping and starting ¼" from pin-marked end points. Repeat to sew all four border strips to quilt.

quilt front

**5.** Fold corner of quilt diagonally, right sides together, matching seams and borders. Place a long ruler along fold line extending across border. Draw a diagonal line across border from fold to edge of border. This is the stitching line. Starting at ¼" mark, stitch on drawn line. Check for squareness, then trim excess. Press seam open.

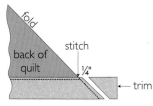

fold

stitch

back of quilt

¼"

← trim

## Layering the Quilt

**1.** Cut backing and batting 4" to 8" larger than quilt top.

**2.** Lay pressed backing on bottom (right side down), batting in middle, and pressed quilt top (right side up) on top. Make sure everything is centered and that backing and batting are flat. Backing and batting will extend beyond quilt top.

**3.** Begin basting in center and work toward outside edges. Baste vertically and horizontally, forming a 3"–4" grid. Baste or pin completely around edge of quilt top. Quilt as desired. Remove basting.

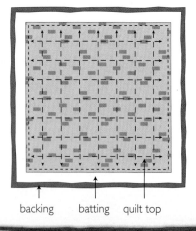

backing    batting    quilt top